The Truth Behind a Series

of Unfortunate Events

Also by Lois H. Gresh

Dragonball Z
The Science of Supervillains
The Science of Superheroes
The Termination Node
Chuck Farris and the Tower of Darkness
Chuck Farris and the Labyrinth of Doom
Chuck Farris and the Cosmic Storm
Technolife 2020
The Computers of Star Trek

The Truth Behind a Series of Unfortunate Events

Eyeballs, Leeches, Hypnotism, and Orphans—
Exploring Lemony Snicket's World

Lois H. Gresh

St. Martin's Griffin ⚲ New York

www.stmartins.com

ISBN 0-312-32703-X
EAN 978-0312-32703-3

First Edition: October 2004

10   9   8   7   6   5   4   3   2   1

To Beagan, the small man who danced at the fire hall: love forever, once desired, love forever, and then you expired.

CONTENTS

This is the book They don't want you to read. It has hip, cool, fun facts about the Lemony Snicket world that you can't get anywhere else. It has games, anecdotes (which means "little stories that allow the author to ramble incoherently for ten minutes"), and little-known references about history and science.

We're going to dig beneath the fiction into the realities of the Snicket universe: Could all of those horrible things really happen to the Baudelaire orphans? If so, how could they happen?

Here are some examples of the miserable topics you'll discover in this book:

What really happens to orphans? What legal rights and types of protection do orphans have? Could someone like the evil Count Olaf really marry the fourteen-year-old Violet?

Is it possible to be allergic to peppermints? What are leeches? What kind of matchbox-sized crab could live in a tin shack at Prufrock Prep? What do crabs eat? What type of fungus—light tan, constantly dripping juice—is growing on the ceiling of the shack? Hypnosis—we'll give you a tell-all chapter that leaves you with real knowledge: Could you be hypnotized (right now, perhaps?), and how would your friends break the spells?

Think of this book as a cool kid's Lemony Snicket Monarch, Cliffs, or Barron's Notes. (Those are books that high school and college kids study so they can pass exams about subjects they know nothing about.)

Think of this book as the Ultimate Book Report about Lemony Snicket.

The Truth Behind a Series

of Unfortunate Events

CHAPTER ONE

Kids Who Invent Things

It was near Desolate Lake in the fall of 1990 that Carolyn Catastrophe planted a shrub that changed the world forever. It was a writhing mass of vines called the Nettle of Frankfurt. Its purple stems were littered with sour berries and flowers that smelled like the sewers.

Carolyn was delighted. By the time the snow melted next April, she and her best friend, Jonquil, would be able to sit beneath the Nettle and cast its berries into the water. The berries would float on the mud and eventually slide into the lower muck of Desolate Lake, where flake-haired horny toads would eat them, gain gas, and belch all those gorgeous bubbles to the surface of the water. "Ah, I can't wait!" Carolyn cried.

Jonquil, who was thirteen, peered at her from beneath his grandfather's cap. "I know the berries are the best for producing toad gas, but, Carolyn, how will we sit beneath the shrub long enough to throw berries into the lake? The Nettle stinks like sewers."

"I've thought of that," said Carolyn, "and it will no longer be a problem. I've invented a solution."

Carolyn could invent most anything. She'd created Liquid Squid Houseplant Fertilizer, which gardeners used all over the world. She'd created a machine that cleaned pollutants from ordinary city air; her Purifying Roto-Whirlers were on the roofs of skyscrapers everywhere.

And now, Carolyn Catastrophe had created a Nettle of Frankfurt that cast only the sweetest pheromones—a word that means "fragrance that makes people dizzy with good thoughts"—across Lake Desolate.

"When we throw berries into the water next April, Jonquil," she said, "people will dance for miles around."

And she was right, for next spring, as the snow melted and the flake-haired horny toads rose from the lake, Carolyn's Nettle blossomed and its aroma filled the air for miles around, and everywhere people stopped fighting and grubbing for money, and people danced together upon the shores of Lake Desolate.

Now in the case of the Baudelaire orphans—Violet, Klaus, and Sunny—life was as bad as the smell of the original Nettle of Frankfurt. Yet life got a little better—just as it did with Carolyn and the people who lived near Lake Desolate—each time Violet invented a contraption to get them out of a jam— a jam, in this case, meaning all those times when the evil Count Olaf tried to kidnap, torture, roast alive, or otherwise hurt the children.

And while Carolyn Catastrophe may or may not be real, and she may or may not be based on the early teenage years of the author—and while there may or may not be a Nettle of Frankfurt on the banks of Lake Desolate, nor any flake-haired horny toads (though there may be some gill-footed sapsucking eagles)—there is indeed an underlying truth about the brilliant inventions devised by Violet Baudelaire.

And that underlying truth is that Violet's inventions could indeed be real, and that you, the reader of this dreadful book, could indeed make her inventions yourself.

In this chapter, we'll take a look at some of Violet's inventions and tell you how to make them. We'll also have fun pondering Violet's more unusual creations, and we'll introduce you to some of the real world's youngest inventors of really cool stuff.

First Up: How to Build a Telephone

Do you remember how Aunt Josephine tells the orphans in *The Wide Window* (Book the Third) that the telephone is a very dangerous device because it can electrocute people? Klaus insists that the telephone is quite safe. And, of course, Violet declares that she's built a telephone and would be happy to take apart Aunt Josephine's telephone to explain how it works. This way, figures Violet, Aunt Josephine will no longer be afraid of telephones.

While reading the book, did you wonder how Violet might build her telephone? Well, I did, and so I read a lot of books and papers about telephones. And then I thought about the telephone for a few weeks. I wondered if Violet created a regular telephone or a cellular one.

I was interested to learn that a man named Elisha Gray invented a telephone around the same time that the more famous Alexander Graham Bell invented the telephone. Each man zoomed to the patent office, but Bell got there first—literally, within hours of Gray's arrival—and after a lengthy legal battle, Bell was given credit as the true inventor of the telephone. In fact, I thought this stuff was so interesting that I wrote about it for you in "Fascinating Tidbit #1" (see box at right).

.But, for now, let's get back to Violet and how she might have built her telephone.

A telephone is actually a simple device. It has a speaker near your ear and a microphone near your mouth. The speaker is tiny and might cost fifty cents. The microphone

Fascinating Tidbit #1:
Who Really Invented the Telephone?

Everyone thinks that Alexander Graham Bell was the one and only inventor of the telephone. This is what we all learned in school.

But this is not quite accurate.

During the 1870s, when Bell patented his telephone, another guy named Elisha Gray created a telephone, too. After a long legal battle, Bell won the right to proclaim himself inventor of the telephone.

In addition, a German named Phillip Reis began working on a telephone in 1860 when he was twenty-six years old. Reis's telephones used delicate diaphragms to transmit sound, and sometimes these diaphragms transmitted nothing more than static. Sadly, at age forty, Reis died, two years before Bell patented the telephone.

And even before Reis, in 1854, the French scientist Bourseul wrote a paper that explained how to transmit speech. Bourseul's method, which used diaphragms, was also used by Reis, and later Gray, and even later, Bell.

Bell's creation of the telephone began with the telegraph, an older method of sending electrical signals over wires. The telegraph used Morse code, in which dots and dashes spelled words. And the telegraph could only send one message over the wire at a single time.

Bell wanted to make a better telegraph. He knew a lot about musical sounds, and we all know that in music many sounds come together and congeal to form harmony. Bell dreamed of a wire that could transmit multiple messages, just as music transmits multiple sounds all at once.

Bell hooked up with electrician Thomas Watson, and by 1876, they created a device that could transmit speech electrically over a wire. The first words uttered over the telephone were Bell's request to Watson, who was in another room: "Mr. Watson, come here, I want you."

When he invented the telephone, Alexander Graham Bell was only twenty-nine years old.

can be made of carbon granules pressed between two thin pieces of metal. As you talk, sound waves compress and decompress the granules.

A simple telephone also has a hook switch, which connects you to the telephone network—the big cables that run from your home to the road to the telephone boxes and to the telephone company.

If you tap the hook switch, you can dial telephone numbers. For example, if you tap the switch twice, the telephone company thinks you have dialed the number two. Violet's telephone could be as simple as this one. And it wouldn't take much for you to make a telephone, too.

Now, it's highly unlikely that Violet created a cell phone. That's a much harder task than building the simple phone described above. To make a cell phone, she would probably need equipment such as a circuit board, a liquid crystal display, a tiny keyboard, a microphone, a speaker, an antenna, and a battery.

There are a lot of other things that Violet invents or builds. Printing presses, hot-air balloon mobile homes, automatic harmonicas, and noisy shoes.

While I'd really like to talk about the noisy shoes first, you might prefer more intellectual topics, such as how to build a hot-air balloon mobile home. So we'll start with that topic first.

Second Up: How to Build a Hot-Air Balloon Mobile Home

In Book the Seventh, *The Vile Village*, the Baudelaire orphans end up in the town of V.F.D., which is filled with old people and crows. Also in V.F.D. is Hector, the town handyman. Due to town Rule #67, which prohibits anyone from building or using mechanical devices, Hector is forced to keep his inventing studio outside of town. There, he has built a hot-air balloon mobile home. Twelve baskets hang from several balloons, and each basket serves as a separate room in Hector's house.

While it might be hard to route plumbing around twelve baskets and install a water tank somewhere, and while it might be hard to build electromagnetic generators for a gigantic engine, it is possible to build a simple hot-air balloon. And if you make twelve of these hot-air balloons and then tie them together, you might indeed end up with a home very similar to Hector's. If you keep enough supplies on hand, such as bread, peanut butter, cookies, maybe some dried bananas and orange soda, your hot-air balloon mobile home would be fairly self-sustaining. The tricky stuff would be plumbing, heat, cooking, and, for lack of a better way to write it, the bathroom facilities. It's hard to figure how Violet might have fixed the plumbing and electromagnetic engine generator, whatever that is, in Hector's home.

So instead, let's ponder how Hector might build his hot-air balloon mobile home. First, just how do these balloons work?

You probably recall from science class that hot air rises over cooler air. This is because hot air is lighter than cold air.

A cubic foot of air weighs approximately one ounce, or twenty-eight grams. When heated, that same cubic foot of air weighs less. If you heat the air to 100 degrees Fahrenheit, it will weigh about one-quarter less, or approximately seven grams less, than it did before you heated it. In a hot-air balloon, each cubic foot of air is light enough to lift approximately seven grams of the basket below.

Think about how enormous a hot-air balloon is. Let's say one of Hector's basket-rooms is about 1,000 pounds. To lift this one basket-room, a hot-air balloon has to contain roughly 65,000 cubic feet of hot air. That's a lot of hot air!

And then, to keep his hot-air balloon and basket-room rising into the clouds, Hector has to keep the air heated at all times. To do this, he puts a burner beneath what's called an open balloon envelope. If the air in the balloon starts cooling and the balloon starts dropping, Hector can reheat the air by firing up his burner. Or in Hector's case, he can reheat the air in twelve balloons using a fancy electromagnetic engine generator.

Suppose Hector is in his basket-room along with compressed liquid propane stored in cylinders. Hoses draw the liquid from the cylinders to the burners, and then the heat turns the liquid propane into hot gas, which rises into the balloon. This is how the hot air remains hot inside the balloon. For a couple of interesting and little-known facts about hot-air balloons, see "Fascinating Tidbit #2" (box on page 10).

Now if *you* want to make a hot-air balloon, I have the instructions. To put them in this book would take about fifteen pages, and most of you would fall asleep, skim that part, or get mad at me for sticking instructions like that into this book. So I'm going to limit myself, hard as that is to do, to giving you some insight as to how Hector and Violet might make the twelve basket-room hot-air balloon mobile home work. How's that for a compromise?

Basically, twelve balloons are strung up together using some loosely connected rope. These balloons are bobbing in the sky, jostling gently against one another. One of the middle balloon basket-rooms contains a command center with battery-driven control systems. These control systems monitor and operate the other balloon basket-rooms in Hector's giant hot-air balloon mobile home. One of these balloon baskets-rooms serves as Hec-

Fascinating Tidbit #2:
Little-Known Facts About
Hot-Air Balloons

Question: Who made the very first hot-air balloon trip in history?

Answer: In 1783, Joseph and Etienne Montgolfier loaded a sheep, a duck, and a chicken into a hot-air balloon, and sent them off for a ride. The balloon was powered by burning straw and manure. King Louis XVI was very impressed, and he started wondering whether people could travel in hot-air balloons.

Question: Who made the very first hot-air balloon trip around the world?

Answer: It's interesting that the very first hot-air balloon trip around the world occurred in 2002. Steve Fossett circled the Earth alone and landed in South Australia. It took him less than one month to make his journey, and he traveled about sixty miles per hour most of the time, though over the Indian Ocean, strong winds propelled his hot-air balloon at speeds of up to two hundred miles per hour.

tor's bedroom. This basket has pillows, blankets, maybe Hector's stuffed gorilla, and some straw on the floor. And another balloon basket-room serves as the kitchen. Here, the basket contains tubs of water with hoses, pouches of dry food, plates, cups, and other items. In short, each room has a different purpose, and all together, they form a hot-air balloon mobile home.

Third Up: How to Create Noisy Shoes

The noisy shoes are in Book the Fifth, *The Austere Academy*. Now this invention of Violet's sounds quite easy to create. She suggests simply gluing pieces of metal on shoes, so the crabs in the tin shack can hear the orphans walking around and the crabs might hide. This sounds very reasonable, don't you think?

Real-life noisy shoes usually do have metal or other hard objects on them. Tap dancers wear noisy shoes, for example. Sometimes, the metal is screwed onto the shoes with an underlying fiberboard cushion.

Oddly enough, ballerina slippers, which are not supposed to be noisy, are some of the hardest shoes around. Given how hard they are, it's actually amazing that ballerinas make such little noise when they dance.[1] Ballerina slippers are probably

---

1. If I were to wear ballerina shoes, I would fall constantly. This would make so much noise that even the hardest, most noisy shoes wouldn't be heard.

a lot more uncomfortable than metal-plated tap shoes. Most pointe ballet shoes are constructed from leather, burlap, paper, glue, and nails. The dancer's weight rests entirely on the oval-shaped platform at the toes. Beneath the shoe is a stiff insole, or shank. As you might imagine, these shoes are *really* stiff when they're new.

Fourth Up: How to Build an Automatic Harmonica

Our final subject—though we could fill an entire book with inventions and machines created by Violet and other characters—is that of the automatic harmonica. You're probably thinking: Of all possible inventions, why did Lois choose this one?

Well, do you know what an automatic harmonica is? I had to think about it for a very long time. And then I still couldn't figure it out. But you might be a lot smarter than I am, and so, if you already know everything about automatic harmonicas, then you can just skip this part and move to the next section of the book.

Yeah, so I chose the automatic harmonica as a topic because I wanted to find out what it is!

Call me stupid. (But not to my face, please. For a photo of my face—so if you ever see me, you'll know who I am and you won't call me stupid—see the "About the Author" at the end of this book.)

The 1928 Tonk Brothers Catalog features an automatic harmonica, which it describes as a "rollmonica" that plays "a music roll just like a player piano. All you have to do is insert a roll and turn the handle while you blow." According to the Virtual Harmonica Museum, rolls for two hundred songs were available for purchase at $1.50 each.[2]

Automatic harmonicas are a lot like player pianos, which, as noted in the Tonk Brothers Catalog, use music rolls and some kind of air flow. In the case of the harmonica, the air is from your mouth. In the case of a player piano, it comes from the pumping of bellows in the bottom of the piano. The pumping causes suction, which makes the piano keys go down and the music roll turn.

For each note the automatic harmonica (or piano) plays, there is a tiny pneumatic bellows. When suction occurs inside the pneumatic bellows, it collapses and you hear a note. The more air you blow into the automatic harmonica, the louder the note. A valve connected to the pneumatic makes it turn off and on.

Now I may be wrong, but it doesn't seem like a simple matter to build one of these things. While Violet could quite easily build a simple telephone, and while Violet and Hector could construct their hot-air balloon mobile home with some effort, it might be tricky for Violet to invent an automatic harmonica.

Snicket, a man we can never trust, of course, tells us in Book the Third, *The Wide Window*, that Violet invented an

---

2. See www.bluesharp.ca/museum.

automatic harmonica before she became an orphan. Given how wealthy the Baudelaire parents were, it's possible that Violet had access to soldering irons, acid baths, metal pastes, dry cells, solutions of hot washing soda, bunsen burners, silver nitrate, potassium bitartrate, powdered chalk, nickel ammonium sulfate, and other tools and substances. It's possible that she could have purchased ancient musical rolls from eBay. Hey, you know what I think? My guess is that Violet did indeed invent an automatic harmonica, but it was big and sort of like a miniature player piano. She could have refurbished this player piano to use air rather than foot pedals. By blowing into a long tube on the side of the player piano, air would force the pneumatic bellows to compress and play notes. It would be like a harmonica and piano all rolled into one weird, new musical instrument. And it wouldn't require soldering irons, acid baths, metal pastes, dry cells, solutions of hot washing soda, bunsen burners, silver nitrate, potassium bitartrate, powdered chalk, or nickel ammonium sulfate.

That's just my thought on the subject, but I'm not nearly as smart as Lemony Snicket.

Last Up: Real-World Kids Who Invent Stuff

It's amazing how many of the truly great inventions have been made by kids. Throughout history, children and teenagers have supplied the world with earmuffs, crutches, cattle-feeding machines, biodegradable disposable diapers, baby spill-proof bowls, and all sorts of computer technology. And that's just a tiny sample of what real-world kids have invented. In real life, Violet Baudelaire would win major science and invention competitions. She'd probably get a full scholarship to Harvard or MIT.

Let's take a look at a few examples of real-life inventors who made amazing things as kids.

Earmuffs? They were invented by Chester Greenwood when he was fifteen years old. In 1873, Chester grew tired of wrapping his head in scarves while iceskating. So he made two ear-shaped loops using wire. His grandma sewed fur on the wire loops, and voilà, earmuffs were born. Later, Chester sold his earmuffs to soldiers in World War I. Becoming an extremely wealthy inventor, he eventually owned more than 100 patents.

Awarded a U.S. patent and winning a huge inventor's award, eleven-year-old Tessanie Marek created crutches with adjustable leg supports. Tessanie's invention allows patients to rest their injured legs directly against her crutches, which greatly eases muscle cramps and pains.

Twelve-year-old Justin Riebeling invented a way to feed cattle quickly and more easily. He created a farm wagon that can hold approximately twenty-five gallons of cattle feed. But that's not all: his wagon includes a remotely controlled chute that fills the feed trough while the wagon is moving. Like Tessanie and many other kids, Justin also won an inventor's award.

The biodegradable disposable diaper was invented by seventeen-year-old Rishi Vasudeva. I have no idea how teenagers know how to make corn-based polymer linings and absorbent cellulose inner paddings, but, then, I'm just a goofy writer of goofy books. I do not have an inventor's brain. Rishi's diaper biodegrades—this word means that the diaper just disintegrates, or falls apart, without causing any pollution—within days after a baby wears it.

Okay, here's a really cool invention: the Oops! Proof No-Spill Feeding Bowl for babies. Get ready for this: the inventor, Alexia Abernathy, was eleven years old when she created her spill-proof bowl. Alexia has a patent, and her bowl is manufactured by Little Kids and sold in stores everywhere.

There's little need to delve into all of the computer technology inventions created by children and teenagers. Need we mention Bill Gates, to name one obvious example of early genius?

Sadly, most computer viruses and worms—nasty programs that attack and destroy computer systems by the many millions—are created by teenagers. This happens to be against the law. My computer, the one on which I am writing this book right now, was attacked by a terrible worm only last week. I wish that young computer geniuses would put their brains to better use. I wish they would invent a way to prevent worms and viruses from attacking my computer. I wish they would invent a computer operating system that wouldn't crash all the time, or maybe a way to install software that doesn't make me go totally bonkers. Someday, it will come. Someone like Violet will put her mind to these matters and make great inventions to make my writing life a lot easier. I'm just waiting . . .

Hey, take a look at "Fascinating Tidbit #3" (see box on page 18), where I tell you about some more real-life kids who invented amazing things. Then I think it's time for some fun, so the next chapter will be about really bad grammar.[3]

---

3. And what could be more fun than grammar?

Fascinating Tidbit #3: Really Cool Kid Inventors

Margaret Knight could easily be in a Lemony Snicket book. As a child of only nine years old, Margaret worked in a cotton mill. (It wouldn't surprise me if she was forced to debark wood as an infant. Child labor laws have really changed over the years. Lots of kids worked really long hours in the old days. In fact, this book has a whole chapter about child labor.)

Anyway, Margaret was totally amazing. In the cotton mill, she saw a steel-tipped shuttle fly off a loom and hurt another worker. Margaret invented a device to keep shuttles from flying off looms.

Later in 1870-71, Margaret invented a machine to make grocery bags. These square-bottomed grocery bags are still used today.

Margaret also invented clasps for robes, numbering machines, window frames, and a rotary engine.

Another one of my favorite stories is that of Becky Schroeder. When she was ten, she started wondering how people could write in the dark. At fourteen, she put phosphorescent paint under her paper, and this invention is still being used in hospitals to read patients' charts at night. In fact, both NASA and the Navy wanted to buy her invention. Phosphorescence, by the way, refers to materials that glow in the dark after being exposed to light.

CHAPTER TWO

Really Bad Grammar

Just pretend that Aunt Josephine is sitting there with you. She's drilling you with grammar questions. When you're done, check your answers and tally your points. Don't worry. These questions are all fun, and some are actually pretty silly.

Let's see how well you do!

1. What is the subject of the following sentence?
   Drowning your daughter in the water is a very bad
   thing to do.
   a. Drowning
   b. daughter
   c. water is a very bad thing
   d. Drowning your daughter in the water

2. Reading this book had a terrible _____ on poor
   Emma.
   a. affect
   b. effect
   c. iffect
   d. uhfect

3. The Handbook for Advanced Sentence Structure is
   more interesting _____ The Tome of Ancient
   Grammar.
   a. thin
   b. then
   c. than
   d. thun

4. Identify the subject, verb, direct object, and indirect
   object in the following sentence.
   Dan gave his sister a caterpillar on the nose.
   Subject: _____

Verb: _____
Direct Object: _____
Indirect Object: _____

5. What is wrong with the following sentence?
   There's a giant gorilla in a seashell rampaging through
   the gas station.
   a. It is really stupid.
   b. It was obviously written by a moron.
   c. Gorillas do not wear seashells. They only wear
      ballgowns.
   d. It came from the brain of a wretch.
   e. All of the above.

6. What is the verb in the following sentence?
   There's a monster raging through my attic.
   a. attic
   b. is
   c. raging
   d. is raging

7. What is wrong with the following sentence?
   The kind man leeched off his wife, then sucked her
   blood for money.
   a. You cannot suck somebody's blood to get money.
   b. The man is obviously evil, not kind.
   c. Leeches are not our friends.

    d. This question has nothing to do with grammar.

    e. All of the above.

8. What is wrong with Uncle Arthur's grammar in the following sentence?

   "We must save each of our gold fishes!" cried Uncle Arthur.

   a. He should be saying, "We must save all of our goldfishes!"

   b. He should be saying, "We must all die now!"

   c. He should be saying, "We ain't gonna save nobody's goldfishes!"

   d. None of the above.

9. What is wrong with the grammar in the following paragraph?

   I had lain on the sofa for hours, when I got up and lied the book on the shelf. Men were lying pipe outside. Chickens were laying eggs. I will lay down now.

   a. I laid the book on the shelf.

   b. Men were laying pipe outside.

   c. I will lie down now.

   d. I had laid on the sofa for hours.

   e. Chickens were lying eggs.

   f. I will lain down now.

   g. I lyed the book on the laid pipe.

   h. a, b, c are correct.

i. d, e, f are correct.

j. g, a, b are correct.

10. Read Question #9 and weep. If you shed even one tear, give yourself two points.

Answers:

1. If you chose d, give yourself three points. If you chose c, give yourself one point.

2. If you chose b, give yourself five points. If you chose d, stick your face in the toaster.

3. If you chose c, give yourself three points. If you chose b, sign up for Latin class next year, drink twelve gallons of water every day until Latin class begins, and develop a strong craving for meatballs.

4. If you get this one right, give yourself ten points.
   Subject: Dan
   Verb: gave
   Direct Object: caterpillar on the nose
   Indirect Object: sister

5. If you chose e, you get a whopping three points. If you chose anything else, you immediately fail this grammar test.

6. If you chose d, *woo hoo*, you are brilliant and you get six points. If you chose a, have your best friend tweak your nose three times and call you a loser. Any other answer, weep for shame and award yourself zero points.

7. If you chose e, you will live a long and very success-ful life. Give yourself two points. If you chose a or c, but pondered b and d for more than two minutes, you will watch sitcom reruns for eternity, and a gray parrot will roost on your head for three months.

8. If you chose a, then you remember Uncle Arthur very well indeed (how did you do that given that Uncle Arthur doesn't really exist?); give yourself ten points. If you chose anything else, read all the Lemony Snicket books again, then try taking this test.

9. If you chose h, you have the patience of a saint, and you get ten points. If you chose anything else, give yourself one point for trying.

10. If you read Question #9 and shed at least one tear, award yourself two points. If you did not read the question, you get zero points. If you shed no tears, or if you shed only one tear, you get zero points. If your tears gushed, dripped, or leapt off your face, give yourself an extra six points. If you shed one tear but the second tear dripped into your mouth, give up now: crawl into bed, pull the covers over your head, and dream about frogs.

Now add all your points. When you have a total, read your fortune below. This fortune is guaranteed by oat companies everywhere to be accurate, 100 percent bogus, and totally punctilious—that is, precise about the most minute details of your future existence.

40 to 58 points: Your awe-inspiring genius will help you solve at least one of the world's problems. Either you will cure the common cold, or you will transform peanuts into roses and mud into penicillin.

21 to 39 points: Your hard work will pay off. Within hours of taking this test, you will have dozens of new friends, be elected a sports captain, and get free cookies. Another option is that, within decades, you will learn how to clean public rest rooms better than anyone else on the staff.

11 to 20 points: You will enjoy a happy, prosperous life as a fast-food burger flipper. You will retire after fifty years of service at Manny's Vat O' Grease.

2 to 10 points: If you try extra hard, you will learn to blow bubbles with gum.

0 to 1 point: Give up now, you loser.

CHAPTER THREE

What Happens to Real Orphans?

What happens to children when they become orphans? What legal rights and types of protection do orphans have? Is it possible for orphans to be sent to lumbermills, academies, and guardian villages?

First of all, let's define the word *orphan*. The word itself is derived from ancient Latin and Greek words that mean "bereaved," which in turn means "mourning the death of someone close to you."

It might seem very obvious that an orphan is a kid whose parents are both dead; but basically, many questions arise from this simple statement. For example, are you technically an orphan if one of your parents is alive but wants nothing to do with you? Are you an orphan if both your parents are deceased but you have one or more grandparents, aunts, uncles, or adult cousins willing to take you in? In fact, is it the law that other family members, such as grandparents, aunts, uncles, or adult cousins, must take you in if your parents are deceased? Is this what happens to the Baudelaire children?

Well, not exactly. Violet, Klaus, and Sunny's parents both die in the fire. Their parents' will specified that Mr. Poe, the banker, would be the keeper of all the children's money should the children become orphans. Poe would keep the Baudelaire fortune tucked away until Violet became a legal adult. Not wanting to raise the children himself, Poe shuffles the children from one horrible home to another, pushing the Baudelaire orphans from one relative to another, and finally, into a so-called guardian village. Of course, Count Olaf wants to be the legal guardian of all that money and will stop at nothing, not even murder, to satisfy his insatiable greed.

Hey, I know that I'm using some big words in this book, but it's all in keeping with the Snicket tradition, you know? Insatiable, in this case, means something like "Count Olaf's greed has no bounds and is limitless" or perhaps "Count

Olaf's hunger for money is similar to the thirst a man feels after he's been lost in the desert for months." Insatiable means "can't get enough."

But enough of that. Let's get back to orphans and what happens with the Baudelaires and Mr. Poe.

The official definition of an orphan (from the National Adoption Information Clearinghouse) is a "minor child whose parents have died, have relinquished their parental rights, or whose parental rights have been terminated by a court."

In most societies, parents and grandparents feel obligated to support children. If your mother dies, then your father is supposed to take care of you. And vice versa. If both parents pass away, then grandparents are supposed to step in and take care of you.

The notion that children really need care, regardless of whether parents are alive or dead, whether grandparents or uncles have an interest in taking care of them, is a long-standing community idea. In the Bible, for example, we learn that orphans, strangers, and widows should share excess food from the harvests (Deuteronomy, xxiv, verse 21). Also in the Bible, we learn that God is the "father of orphans," meaning his food harvest must be shared with them (Psalms, lxvii, 6).

But treatment of the poor, including orphans, has generally not been good. For example, the ancient Romans did not officially support widows and orphans. And while orphanages were thought to be charitable institutions as opposed to places of horror, many orphanages throughout history were indeed the stuff of nightmares.

However, even in ancient Rome, as Christianity took root, charity became more acceptable. Hospitals were established for the sick, for poor children, and, specifically, for orphans. These early orphan hospitals were called *orphanotrophia*.

Later, around the world, orphanages became common. In 1548, the first orphanage was built in North America, when the Spanish established a Mexican orphanage for girls only. I do not know what the Mexicans and Spanish did, if anything, for the orphan boys. In what is now the United States, the first orphanage was established in 1727 by French king Louis XV. Between 1855 and 1898, fifty-one orphanages were established throughout England, Ireland, and Scotland.

But as noted earlier, orphanages have never been places of joy for children. And the misery of orphans is well known.

In 1758, the English created workhouses for their orphans. Even little kids became slave laborers in these workhouses, and their overall living conditions were abominable (that means "awful").

The lives of the three Baudelaire orphans are very similar to the lives of orphans in England during the 1700s and 1800s. The Baudelaires are also sent to workhouses. They slave away in lumber mills, in schools, in offices. They work as handymen for a guardian village.

The Baudelaires are also much like the orphans in the novels of Charles Dickens. These novels are very famous, and if

Orphan Stories

Despite horrible childhoods, many orphans are able to do wonderful things in the world. Like the Baudelaires, they rise from wretched circumstances and make the world a better place. Here are some examples.[1]

Faith Hill. She grew up as an orphan in Mississippi. Now, she is an extremely famous singer who has won Grammy awards and sold many millions of records.

Tom Monaghan. An orphan from Michigan, Tom is the founder and chief executive officer of Domino's Pizza. He has said that his inspiration was Abraham Lincoln, the poor farm boy who grew up to be president of the United States.

Andrew Jackson. Orphaned at fourteen, he grew up to be president of the United States.

Robert B. Macon. Orphaned at nine, he grew up to be a United States representative from Arkansas.

Josiah Belden. Orphaned at fourteen, he was the first mayor of San Jose, California.

Austin Church. Orphaned as a young child in the early 1800s, he attended Yale Medical School and invented the notion of using bicarbonate of soda in baking.

John T. Cutting. Orphaned at ten, he grew up to be a congressman.

---

1. The examples of Faith Hill, Tom Monaghan, and many others, are on the Web site www.orphanconnect.com.

you haven't been forced to read them in school yet, you might want to read them anyway.

As for real orphans in the United States, the Americans were treating orphans much the same way as the English. Almshouses (a word for "poorhouses") were established for both children and adults. In 1875, New York allowed children who were more than three years old and who were "not defective" to leave the poorhouses and to go instead to orphan asylums. Later, children who were older than two got to leave the poorhouses and live in orphan asylums.

Why were there so many orphan asylums during the late 1800s? Because in the mid-1800s, the Industrial Revolution was in an upswing. People flocked to big cities, where they found crime, long working hours, sickness, and poverty. Many mothers died in childbirth or from sickness. Many children were forced to live on the streets. As early as 1850, New York had twenty-seven orphan asylums, and yet New York still had approximately 10,000 street orphans with no place to go. And so, by the late 1800s, there was a huge need to *do* something: and orphan asylums boomed.

From the mid-1800s through World War I, many orphans were shipped on "orphan trains" to farms in the American west to work. A two-year-old boy might be shipped to Kansas, while his four-year-old brother was shipped to Missouri.

Nowadays, orphans have a little more protection. They no longer live in workhouses and eat gruel, for example. They are not sent to guardian villages. They are not sent on orphan trains to Kansas. It is illegal to make babies strip tree bark in lumbermills. It is illegal to make babies work in school offices. Adoption agencies are constantly trying to place orphans into good homes.

Still, the plight of most orphans remains dire. Around the world, many orphans have AIDS, for example, and there simply is no place for them to go. While some foster homes are good places for orphans, many are wretched places; and orphans move from one foster home to another, often living in twenty, forty, or more homes before reaching the age of eighteen.

We can only hope that things improve.

CHAPTER FOUR

Are You as Smart as
Violet and Klaus?

This chapter poses questions that test your memory of Violet's and Klaus's knowledge. We're also going to ask a few other questions, and at the end of the chapter, we'll give you all the right answers. Then you can decide for your-self if you're as smart as Violet and Klaus.

Of course, if you get a really bad score and miss all the

questions, remember that you're reading a truly lousy book written by a miserable author with no skill. In other words, despite a score of 0.00 percent, you may be quite intelligent and possess a magnificent memory.

Perhaps in my current state, a condition that I cannot bear to tell you about, I am incapable of writing questions that any sane person can answer. Had my father not pinned his crimes on me, had the authorities not caught up with me in San Orleando that hot summer before I started second grade, had I learned how to read and write in a school rather than in a chicken factory, well, this book might be worth reading and the questions in this chapter might have real answers.

But this is all we have, dear readers, so bear with me. I feel that somewhere through the ether—which does not really exist—Lemony Snicket is shouldering some of my woes and urging me onward . . .

A Series of Five Questions

These are questions posed in the Lemony Snicket books, and Violet and/or Klaus know the answers to these questions. I even think that Sunny knows some of these answers. Anyway, because these questions are in the Snicket books, I pose them in a series, which means a group of things that all belong together for some reason.

To make things easier for you, I'm giving multiple choice answers for each question. You need only choose the correct option. Easy, huh? And for every answer you get right in this series, you get whopping big points.

Crocodiles Versus Alligators

1. How does a crocodile differ from an alligator?
   a. There are no differences between a crocodile and an alligator.
   b. Crocodiles have an overbite, whereas alligators have no dental problems.
   c. Crocodiles eat humans and sheep, whereas alligators only eat humans.
   d. The most common difference known by people is that crocodiles have narrow snouts, whereas alligators have round snouts.
   e. Crocodiles are bright green, whereas alligators are neon purple.

Cool Facts. In case you need help with the first question, here are some facts about crocodiles and alligators. If you read this stuff, you can get the answer right.

- **Snout and Skull.** This is the difference most often cited by people. Alligators have rounded snouts and skulls. Crocodiles have narrow snouts with pointed skulls.

- **Color.** Alligators are grayish-black. Crocodiles are grayish-green. Both colors absorb sun well, and keep the animals cooler.

- **Where They Live.** Alligators live in cooler climates than crocodiles. Also, alligators live primarily in fresh water. Crocodiles like saltwater and they really like the heat, so they're found in places like Africa, South America, Australia, and southeastern Asia. The only place in the world where both crocodiles and alligators live together is in the Everglades in Florida.

- **Nests.** Alligators build mounds for their nests, whereas crocodiles dig holes for their eggs.

- **Eating People.** It is rare for an alligator to eat a person. Crocodiles, on the other hand, are more familiar with humans and recognize us as food.

- **Dental Problems.** Alligators have an overbite. What this means is that all of the alligator's top teeth come down over its bottom teeth, so when the alligator shuts its giant mouth, you see a bunch of top teeth sticking out. When crocodiles shut their giant mouths, you can see both top and bottom teeth.

- **Different "Official" Families.** Scientists place crocodilians into three different families. The *alligatoridae* include both alligators and caimans. The *crocodylidae* contains the crocodiles. And finally, the *gavialidae* includes the gharial.

During the Mesozoic era (approximately 240 million years ago), reptiles ruled the Earth. Alligators, crocodiles, caimans, and gharials—collectively known as *crocodilians*—are the only animals alive today who date all the way back to the Meso-zoic era. All crocodilians are similar in that they have huge bodies, mouths, teeth, and tails.

In the southeastern United States, Spanish explorers came across these prehistoric-looking lizards and called them *el la-garto*, which means . . . surprise! . . . "lizard." This term was shortened by English settlers to *allagarto*, which later be-came . . . surprise! . . . alligator.

Alligators and crocodiles have webbed hind feet, which help the giant lizards maneuver through the water, much as ducks steer. However, unlike ducks, the giant lizards have long toes on each front foot. And unlike ducks, alligators and crocodiles have giant teeth, eat animals, and well . . . other than the webbed feet, there isn't much hope that a duck and an alligator will ever be best friends.

How many teeth does an alligator have? Eighty, and each is very long and sharp. In fact, if an alligator loses a tooth (maybe an angry duck yanks one out?), a replacement tooth will pop from the lizard's gum. But he only has one replacement for each tooth. This is kind of gross, but the alligator doesn't chew the animals it devours. It just swallows prey whole or in huge wads.

Alligators can actually survive for long periods in freezing water. They keep their nostrils above the water surface to breathe. But even if they are trapped completely beneath the ice—including their nostrils—they can survive for as long as eight hours without taking even one breath. Their body slows way down, so it requires little air.

How do crocodilians talk to each other? Actually, they say a lot, and some can communicate up to twenty different messages to their buddies. A low cough or hiss, for example, means that a crocodilian is feeling slightly threatened. A high-intensity hiss with a bite means that a crocodilian is feeling extremely threatened. When a male is interested in a female, he bellows once, but his one bellow sounds more like thunder rolling in over the swamps than a mere woof from a dog.

The largest crocodilian in the world is called *Crocodylus porosus*, which can grow nearly twenty feet long and up to 3,310 pounds—yes, that's approximately one and a half tons.

There are many types of crocodilians in the world. Specifically, there are two alligators (the American and Chinese), fourteen crocodiles, six caimans, and one species of gharial.

The female American alligator can reach six to eight feet long, and the male can be sixteen feet long. By contrast, in prehistoric times, the crocodilian measured as much as sixty feet in length.

The Chinese alligator rarely grows longer than seven feet. Its head is shorter than the head of the American alligator, and the Chinese gator has big bony plates over its eyes and also on its belly. The Chinese gator is black with yellow bands on its body.

The Nile crocodile is well known in movies and novels as a beast that eats people. This is probably because these movies and novels are set in the African jungle during exciting adventures down the Nile River. However, in reality, the Nile crocodile does eat large animals, such as antelope, hippos, buffalo, and large cats. And in reality, they probably do kill more people than all other types of crocodilians combined.

The one species of gharial is in India. Its name is derived from the word *gavialis,* which comes from the Hindi word *ghariyal,* which means "crocodile." It has a long, narrow snout with a bulbous growth on the end. It has anywhere from 106 to 110 teeth, quite a bit more than alligators and crocodiles.

There are many differences, as you've seen, between alligators and crocodiles. And we've only touched on the subject. Most likely, Klaus knows about all the other differences as well, such as the fact that crocodiles and gharials have salt glands on their tongues, whereas alligators and caimans do not. But basically, you get the point.

Let's move on to our next Klaus question.

Julius Ceasar
2. Who killed Julius Caesar?
   a. Antony
   b. Shakespeare
   c. Brutus
   d. Cleopatra
   e. The Nile crocodile

Hints. In case you need help with this question—such as who was this guy, and why does Klaus care who killed him?—here are some facts about Julius Caesar. If you wade through my drivel, you will be able to answer the question correctly.

The author of the *Julius Caesar* play, William Shakespeare, was born in 1564 in England. His father was a glove maker, and after attending elementary school, Shakespeare left his formal education behind. He wrote thirty-seven plays and more than 150 sonnets, and eventually, Shakespeare became the most famous playwright in English history.

Shakespeare wrote the *Julius Caesar* play in 1599 in London. The story itself is set in 44 B.C. in ancient Rome. As the Roman empire grew in power, military leaders and senators stopped at nothing to become its ruler. Because Julius Caesar was most favored to become Rome's leader, he was at great risk. The play *Julius Caesar* shows us what was happening in Ancient Rome during this time period, and includes the assassination of Caesar, as well as the war that followed his death.

As to who actually killed Julius Caesar, which Klaus professes to know, it is somewhat open to debate. First, I'll give you a big clue:

He was my friend, faithful and just to me.
But Brutus says he was ambitious,
And Brutus is an honourable man.
When that the poor have cried, Caesar hath wept.
Yet Brutus says he was ambitious,
And Brutus is an honourable man.
I thrice presented him a kingly crown,

Which he did thrice refuse. Was this ambition?
Yet Brutus says he was ambitious,
And sure he is an honourable man.

In Act II, Scene ii, a character named Antony speaks these
lines. This happens during Caesar's funeral. It was Brutus,
actually, and his buddies who killed Julius Caesar. Oops. I
gave away the answer. Let me rephrase that: It might have
been Brutus and his buddies who killed Julius Caesar, according to Antony's funeral speech. Why? Antony pre-
tends with these words to think of Brutus as an honorable
man and a great friend of Caesar's. However, Antony goes
on and on, paying ridiculous amounts of respect to Brutus
and his pals, which implies that Antony is actually dissing
them.

If I were to say to you something like this—we'll pretend
that your name is Count Olaf—

"Oh, Count Olaf, what a great man, what an honorable
man. Count Olaf, no man can be greater or more kind, gen-
erous, and law-abiding than you, my dear sir. Truly, no
greater friend of Violet, Klaus, and Sunny ever existed than
you, dear, dear Count Olaf."

—well, clearly, I'd be exaggerating and exhibiting some
heavy sarcasm. My meaning would be clear, that I think very
little of Count Olaf, and I am suggesting strongly that Count
Olaf is indeed no friend at all of the Baudelaires.

That's exactly what Antony is doing in his funeral speech.

Is it possible that someone other than Brutus killed Julius Caesar? After all, a throng of conspirators clusters around Caesar, stabbing him to death. So who *really* did it?

Perhaps Klaus has some special insight into this matter. As I've said before, he's a lot smarter than I am.

But here's how I see it: According to the play, a guy named Casca stabs Caesar first, then everyone else stabs Caesar, and finally, Brutus steps forward and plunges his knife into the dying man. Note that I say, *dying* man. Caesar is not yet dead when Brutus stabs him.

When Caesar sees Brutus, he speaks his last words, "Et tu, Brute?" which means "And you, Brutus?" To speak these words, clearly Caesar must still be alive.

But then he drops dead. Hence, it is Brutus who wields the final blow.

Of course, all the conspirators dealt death blows, and it's possible that the guy before Brutus provided the fatal knife stab. It is possible that Caesar was going to die whether Brutus stabbed him or not.

I bet this is why it's remarkable that Klaus knows who *really* killed Julius Caesar.

Maybe Klaus liked *Julius Caesar* because it's a very cool story, with lots of lightning, walking dead, and lions roaming around the city. Maybe he liked it because the story has undertones about free will versus fate; that is, whether people like Klaus are fated to die at the hands of Count Olaf, or whether they have the free will and strength to rise above being at the mercy of murderous, phony friends.

Battering Ram

3. What is a battering ram?
   a. A large sheep with horns that can pierce metal doors or walls
   b. A large amount of computer random-access memory that can penetrate firewalls
   c. The Royal Academy of Music
   d. A heavy object that is banged against doors or walls to break them down
   e. A large destructive sea goddess

Hints. You're on your own with the battering ram question. You either get it right, or you suffer the consequences and lose vast amounts of critical points. I'm a nice guy, though, so I'll give you a clue: Violet explains what a battering ram is in Book the Seventh, *The Vile Village*.

Tiller

4. What is a tiller?
   a. The front of the boat, where the wind blows hardest
   b. A lever on the top of the boat, where the steering wheel is
   c. Down the hatch, where Count Olaf's whiskey is stored
   d. A batten and a roach combined, and the jib, luff, and leech are splintered beyond repair
   e. It steers the ship by controlling the rudder.

Hints. You're on your own with the tiller question, too. You either get it right, or you suffer the consequences and lose vast amounts of critical points. I'm a nice guy, though, so I'll give you a clue: Violet explains what a tiller is in Book the Third, *The Wide Window*. She, Klaus, and Sunny are in a sailboat during a hurricane. The one truly odd thing about the Snicket tiller is that Violet instructs Sunny to "work the tiller." Sunny is the most remarkable baby ever born.

Optimist

5. What is an optimist?

   a. Someone like Phil in Book the Fourth, *The Miserable Mill*, an optimist always thinks that everything is upbeat, pleasant, and hopeful. For example, when encountering a hungry and very angry Nile crocodile, an optimist might say, "You are the light of my life. Please come and kiss me."

   b. Someone like Phil in Book the Fourth, *The Miserable Mill*, an optimist always thinks that everything is downbeat, nasty, and hopeless. For example, when encountering a hungry and very angry Nile crocodile, an optimist might say, "You are going to eat me alive, I just know it, and I will die a slow and hideous death in your feverish, infected jaws."

   c. Someone like Phil in Book the Fourth, *The Miserable Mill*, an optimist always thinks that he has to examine everyone's eyeballs. For example, when encountering a hungry and very angry Nile crocodile, an optimist might say, "Look at this string of letters. Do you see an E, an A, a T, an M, or an E?"

d. Someone like Phil in Book the Fourth, *The Miserable Mill*, an optimist always thinks that he has to optimize the way everything is done. For example, when encountering a hungry and very angry Nile crocodile, an optimist might say, "Your jaws are not open quite wide enough. It you open them to an angle of 90.52 degrees, you will be able to swallow me in one big piece rather than eat me in chunks."

e. Someone like Phil in Book the Fourth, *The Miserable Mill*, an optimist always sprays heavy, oily mists on everything. For example, when encountering a hungry and very angry Nile crocodile, an optimist might say, "Hold still, dear, while I spray you with this melted pig grease. Oops, I accidentally got pig grease all over myself! No, no, stay back—"

Five Questions Not in a Series

These questions are not in the Lemony Snicket books. It is possible that even kids as smart as Violet and Klaus cannot answer these questions. Because these questions are just randomly posed, they are not in a series. I admit freely that these questions have absolutely nothing in common.

Because these questions are harder than the last ones, for

every answer you get right, you get ten points. If you get these questions right, you are a genius.

6. Do you want your stomach lining cells to die every week?
   a. Yes
   b. No

7. What are the world's largest snakes?
   a. Texas Blind Snake
   b. Sonoran Shovelnose Snake
   c. Big Ol' Kingsnake
   d. Python and Boa
   e. Diamondback Snake

8. What are Komodo Dragons?
   a. Huge fire-breathing monsters on Chinese islands
   b. Tiny lizards that look like dragons
   c. Enemies of Godzilla
   d. Huge lizards that live on Indonesian islands
   e. Komodo Dragons are not real

9. Which Dwarf facts are accurate?
   a. Short
   b. Usually bearded
   c. During the day, cannot appear above the ground
   d. If Dwarfs do exist, which we cannot say for sure, then all three Dwarf facts a to c could be correct.

e. There are no accurate Dwarf facts, because Dwarfs do not really exist.

10. Are plants really chemists in disguise?
   a. Yes
   b. No

All the Answers and Your Score!

1. If you chose d, give yourself three points. If you chose any other answer, give up now and move to the next chapter.

2. If you chose c, give yourself one point. I shouldn't even give you the one point—I mean, after all, I gave you the answer!—but most kids don't care about Julius Caesar at all, whereas they might care a little about alligators and crocodiles, so I figure it this way: If you even bothered to read this question, you deserve one point. If you chose any answer other than c, give yourself zero points.

3. If you chose d, give yourself five points. If you chose any other answer, give yourself zero points.

4. If you chose e, give yourself five points. If you chose any other answer, give yourself zero points.

5. If you chose a, give yourself two points. If you chose any other answer, give yourself one point. There's no logic behind these point values. I'm in a good mood and want to give you one point for a wrong answer. I might

be in a bad mood by the time I write the next question, so in that case, you might get zero points for a correct answer. So take your free point now, as you might need it within the next few minutes.

6. If you chose a, give yourself ten points. Yes, you want your stomach lining cells to die every week. You also want most of the cells that line the inside of your small intestine to die every week. Today alone, a hundred billion red blood cells will die in your liver and spleen. The reason is that many kinds of body cells are actually programmed to age and die. And in the case of some kinds of cells, such as those in your stomach, they exist in such hazardous environments that death is inevitable. When you consider that the cells lining your stomach are bathed in acid all the time, it's a no-brainer that those cells are going to die—frequently. But at any rate, after your body cells die, they are replaced by new, healthy cells, so all this body cell death is good for you. There's actually a word for this process: *apoptosis*.

7. If you chose d, give yourself ten points. In honor of Book the Second, *The Reptile Room*, we'll talk more about giant snakes in the chapter "Strange Snakes, Lizards, and Toads."

8. If you chose d, give yourself ten points. Komodo Dragons are huge lizards that live on Indonesian islands. There are approximately 13,000 Indonesian islands that span about 3,230 miles along the equator. The Dragons are not known to live naturally anywhere else in the

world. Typically, the lizards are sand-colored with dark brown spots. Both their tails and necks are very long. An adult male may grow to approximately eight feet long and may weigh about 150 pounds.

9. If you chose d or e, give yourself ten points.

10. If you chose a, give yourself ten points. Yes, plants are really chemists in disguise. The Earth contains approximately 275,000 species of plants, and each species contains several hundred to several thousand chemicals.[1] In addition, a plant can mix its chemicals into millions of combinations.

Now add all your points. When you have a total, read your intelligence quotient (IQ) results below. These IQ results are guaranteed by The Teachers Association of Greater Mongolian River Tributaries to be accurate, 100 percent false, and completely contradictory. Good luck!

25 to 66 points. Call yourself: Klaus Baudelaire. Okay, let's face it, you are the top of the top, the king of the brains, the epitome of all that is brilliant in the world. You need to put your God-given talents to work. Figure out how to stop war. Find a solution to world hunger, poverty, and while you're at it, the plight of orphans everywhere. Cure cancer—oh, please!—

---

1. Stephen Harrod Buhner, *The Lost Language of Plants* (White River Junction, Vermont: Chelsea Green Publishing Company, 2002), p. 142.

and while you're at it, find a fix for common mold. You can do anything, Klaus.

15 to 24 points. Call yourself: Albert Einstein. Sorry, you didn't score quite high enough to be as smart as Klaus Baudelaire. You'll have to settle for the IQ of Albert Einstein. I know it's a blow, but we have to live with these things.

6 to 14 points. Call yourself: Sunny at the Age of One Month. Don't feel bad. You're still smarter than a writer. It's not saying much, but it beats my lot in life. If I could use my teeth to make staples, believe me, I wouldn't be sitting here, writing this book. If I could use my teeth to debark tree trunks and if I had any clue yet how to use the English language, I'd consider myself lucky.

0 to 5 points. Call yourself: A Professional Writer. Clearly, your intelligence will lead only to one profession in life, that of a writer. You do not have the brain power required to do anything else. Had you scored but one more point, you might have lucked out and grown up to be a junior trainee grave digger or the world's leading collector of ordinary dirt. But alas, it seems that your fate will be the same as mine, and well, I hope you like gruel with a quarter ounce of cheese every now and then.

CHAPTER FIVE

Strange Snakes, Lizards, and Toads

With Book the Second, *The Reptile Room*, in mind, this chapter supplies some facts behind Dr. Montgomery's weird reptiles. Is there such a thing as a Barbary Chewer Snake? How about an Alaskan Cow Lizard or an Irascible Python? What does a herpetologist really do? How does a toad differ from a frog? Is it possible to create mutant reptiles? If so, what would they look like, and would they be dangerous? Does venom differ from snake to snake? Can a snake swallow a person? Can two snakes drive a car? How do real "snake traps" work?

First, what *are* reptiles? Mainly living on land, reptiles are vertebrates, meaning they have backbones, as do mammals (us), fish, and amphibians. They are cold-blooded creatures, and they lay eggs. Most reptiles have waterproof skin coated with scales, and they periodically shed their skin.

There are four types of reptiles: turtles; snakes and lizards; tuataras, which are New Zealand lizardlike creatures; and crocodilians, which we discussed in the last chapter.

Turtles have a bony endoskeleton, which means they have bony skeletons inside their bodies. In addition, turtles have protective shells, into which they can retract their head, arms, legs, and tail.

Snakes are legless reptiles with long bodies. Their backbones consist of an enormous number of bones, which is why snakes slither around, appearing to be boneless. All snakes swallow animals whole, and then their strong stomach juices liquefy the prey. Some snakes coil around an animal and squeeze until the poor animal dies. Others inject their prey with venom, or poison, from their fangs. Worldwide, there are 2,940 different snake species. Most are pretty benign, meaning harmless, but many are deadly. For examples of really deadly snakes, see "The Most Deadly Snakes in the World" (pages 57–60). And if you're curious about the difference between pythons and boa constrictors, take a look at "Pythons and Boas" (pages 62–64).

Lizards generally move more quickly than snakes and turtles. While snakes are legless, most lizards have four legs that give them good balance. They also have long tails. Most lizards eat insects, though some, such as iguanas, eat plants. Worldwide, there are 4,675 different lizard species. For examples of strange lizards, see "Weirdo Lizards in the World" (pages 65–66).

Tuataras, which live on islands in New Zealand, are amphibious reptiles, meaning they can live in water. These reptiles are the only surviving members of the order *Rhyncohocephalia*, which dates back to the Mesozoic era, and they happen to be even more ancient than dinosaurs. Tuataras have a row of spines down the middle of their back and tail. And get this: they have a third eye on top of their heads.

Finally, the crocodilians, as we learned earlier, are meat eaters (or to use the fancy word, they are *carnivores*). They usually have long snouts with very sharp teeth. They have four legs, an extremely long and powerful tail, and a very hard armor of thick scales.

Dr. Montgomery is a herpetologist. It's pretty clear that he studies weird reptiles. But what does a herpetologist *really* do? He studies a wee bit more than reptiles. He also studies amphibians, which are cold-blooded animals with vertebrates, the fancy word for backbones. Speaking of fancy words, you can impress your friends and teachers if you say *poikilothermic* instead of *cold-blooded*. Both words mean the same thing. So what's the difference between an amphibian and a reptile?

Well, amphibians do not have scales like reptiles, and amphibians breed in the water.

Together, reptiles and amphibians are called *herps,* which comes from the Greek *herpeton.* In addition to herpetologists, who study herps, there are herpetoculturists, who breed herps mostly as a hobby.

It's unusual for a herpetologist to study animals on his or her own. (That sort of thing lies more in the domain of the herpetoculturist.) Scientific studies have become so sophisticated that most biology, which includes the subfield of herpetology, requires that people work for universities, corporations, or privately funded research institutes.

Now, speaking of Dr. Montgomery, is there really such a thing as a Barbary Chewer Snake? How about an Alaskan Cow Lizard or an Irascible Python? Well, I'm afraid not—

—though there is such a thing as a Sidewinder Snake that happens to be a favorite food item for Barbary Leopards. If the Barbary Leopard finds the Sidewinder Snake to be chewy, then I suppose a nickname for the Sidewinder Snake might be the Barbary Chewer Snake.

The Alaskan Cow Lizard is an enigma. While I can somehow guess at a possible meaning behind the Barbary Chewer Snake, the Alaskan Cow Lizard remains puzzling.

On the other hand, an Irascible Python makes sense, because pythons tend to be killers and irascible means "really angry and mean."

But Dr. Montgomery also studies amphibians, which include frogs and toads; salamanders and newts; and caecilians, wormlike creatures.

First, let's pretend to be herpetologists and ponder how frogs differ from toads:

- Belonging to the Ranidae family, frogs have slimy, smooth skin; lay eggs in clusters; have webbed hind feet for leaping and swimming; and have two bulging eyeballs. In addition, frogs have small, cone-shaped teeth on their upper jaws, and some even have tiny teeth on the roofs of their mouths.
- Belonging to the Bufonidae family, toads have warty, dry skin; lay eggs in chains; have short hind legs for hopping; and have poison glands behind their eyeballs. What do you think they do with these glands? They use them to squirt poison at their predators. Toads do not have teeth.
- There are approximately 400 species of frogs.
- There are approximately 300 species of toads.

Interesting Little Frog Facts:

- The Goliath frog in West Africa grows to nearly one foot long and often weighs as much as a cat.
- In 190 million years, the body shape and skeleton of frogs has not changed.
- The smallest frog in the southern part of the world is the Brazilian *Psyllophryne didactyla*, also known as the Gold Frog. It is only ⅜ of an inch long.

- The smallest frog in the northern part of the world is called the *Eleutherodactylus iberia,* and it was discovered very recently—in 1996, actually, in Cuba.
- Some poisonous toads can actually kill dogs.
- You know how we have schools of fish, flocks of birds, and herds of cattle? Well, groups of frogs are called *armies* of frogs.

Salamanders and newts are amphibians with tails. They look a little like frogs that happen to have tails and limbs of equal size. Salamanders have smooth skin, while newts have rough skin.

Caecilians are really creepy-looking legless amphibians. They resemble slimy, scaleless snakes. They can be one to two inches round (yuck!) and can be several feet long (double yuck!). They live underground, which is probably a good thing, as I would not want to see these things slithering around my lawn or curling around my legs. It's a good thing that I'm not a herpetologist like Dr. Montgomery, because I don't have the fortitude (that means "strength") to hang around snakes, poisonous toads, and caecilians.

Is it possible to create mutant reptiles? Sure, through what's called genetic engineering.

Genes determine how plants and animals handle poisons, battle infections and other illnesses, digest foods, and respond to environmental conditions. Genes determine what plants and animals look like.

A genetic mutation may be inherited from one or both par-

The Most Deadly Snakes in the World

Of the one to two million snake bites reported each year in the world, approximately 50,000 are deadly. In the United States, only a dozen or so people die each year from snake bites.

To be deadly, a snake needs really toxic venom, which means its venom must kill very quickly. A dangerous snake may bite people a lot but have fairly safe venom. A deadly snake may rarely bite people, and, in reality, be quite docile; but its venom kills on impact.

Dangerous snakes include Coral snakes, which have incredibly toxic venom but which rarely strike people. So the Coral may not be particularly deadly. See the difference?

Some snakes have rear fangs, which are really gigantic rear teeth with grooves. When the snake bites and swallows prey, venom flows down the teeth grooves. Needless to say, these snakes have a fancy scientific name: they are called opisthoglyph snakes. In this category are the Boomslang and Twig snakes, both deadly to humans.

A proteroglyph snake has front fangs that do not retract, spring out, or move in any other way; they are always in the same place in the snake's mouth. To release venom, this type of snake chews its prey. In this category are the Cobra, Krait, Mamba, and Coral snakes—all among the most deadly snakes in the world.

Finally, the solenoglyph snake has very weird front fangs that move. Unlike the fangs of the proteroglyph snake described above, the fangs of the solenoglyph snake actually fold backward and retract into the snake's mouth. When the snake feels like injecting venom, its fangs spring out and pierce the victim's flesh. This type of snake essentially uses its fangs as a series of knives: it opens its mouth 180 degrees with the fangs sticking straight out, then it lunges and stabs the victim with all the fangs. Here we're talking about Rattlesnakes, Gaboon Vipers, and Copperheads.

Listed below are some of the most deadly snakes in the world. There are others, of course, but we have to limit ourselves a bit, or this book would be really long.

Gaboon Viper. Found primarily in East and Central Africa, the Gaboon Viper is the largest snake in Africa. It weighs up to forty-four pounds and its camouflage colors make it difficult to see on the rainforest floor. With the longest fangs in the world, this snake can kill a man within fifteen minutes.

King Cobra. Found in India, Southern China, and Southeast Asia, this snake can grow to be up to eighteen feet long. It bites and sprays its venom, which is powerful enough to kill an elephant.

Death Adder. Found in Australia and New Guinea, the Death Adder is kind of a cross between a viper and a cobra. With only 10 milligrams of its venom required to kill a man, the Death Adder injects as much as 180 milligrams per bite.

Black Mamba. Found in South Africa, this killer grows up to fourteen feet long and has a head shaped like a coffin. The Black Mamba is nearly invulnerable, as its venom can kill almost anything.

Mohave Rattlesnake. Found in the American Southwest, the Mohave Rattlesnake only requires approximately 10 milligrams of venom to kill a man. Each snake bite injects 50 to 90 milligrams of venom, which is twenty times more potent than the venom injected by the Western Diamondback.

Saw-Scaled Viper. Found in Middle Eastern Asia, the Saw-Scaled Viper is the big boy killer of African snakes. Its venom is five times more deadly than cobra venom, and it kills more people every year than all other African snakes combined.

Australian Brown Snake. Native to Australia, this snake can kill you with only one fourteen-thousandth of an ounce of its venom. I wouldn't want to get near one of these guys.

Malayan Krait. Found in Southeast Asia and Indonesia, the Malayan Krait kills 50 percent of people it bites.

Coral Snake. This deadly viper is found in North America. With extremely potent venom, the Coral is mild-mannered and small, and most of them are not able to kill with a single bite.

Inland Taipan. Slithering around Australia, the Inland Taipan is also known as the Fierce Snake, and with good reason. It has the most deadly venom of all snakes. The venom delivered in one Inland Taipan bite contains enough poison to kill one hundred people.

Boomslang. Another African snake, the Boomslang has very long venom fangs and can open its mouth up to 180 degrees wide.

Tiger Snake. This viper kills more Australians than any other snake.

ents. When this happens, the mutation is in almost every cell, and when cells divide, the mutation is reproduced in the new cells. Another term for this type of mutation is a *germline muta-tion*, derived from the notion of germ cells, the egg and sperm.

The term *transgenics* refers to the creation of embryos containing genes from other species. Specifically, "not only can a foreign gene be put into the cells of an organism: the gene can actually be incorporated into the DNA derived from germ cells or embryonic cells of another organism. From this combination, an embryo can be produced that contains this gene that came originally from another species (called a trans-gene). Transgenic embryos can be put into an adult female . . .

which will then give birth to [offspring] permanently carry-ing the transgene."[1]

That's pretty heavy stuff to read,[2] I admit, but the bottom line here is that sure, Dr. Montgomery can create weird mu-tant reptiles such as Alaskan Cow Lizards, Mutant Potato Toads (which I made up), and Corn-Fed Croco-Newts (which I also made up).

As for some of the other questions raised in *The Reptile Room*, here are some quick answers:

Does venom differ from snake to snake? Absolutely. All snakes use venom to capture, kill, and digest prey. However, the types of venom do vary.

For example, hematoxic venom gets into the victim's blood and destroys body tissue. Pit vipers have hematoxic venom. Neurotoxic venom gets into the victim's nervous system and brain. Cobra and coral snakes have neurotoxic venom. For de-tails about various snakes and their venom, see "The Most Deadly Snakes in the World" (pages 57–60).

Can a snake swallow a person? No, but if a pack of wild snakes gangs up on some guy lost in the wilderness, then that

---

1. Frederick B. Rudolph and Larry V. McIntire (editors), *Biotechnology: Science, Engineering, and Ethical Challenges for the 21st Century* (Washington, D.C.: Joseph Henry Press, 1996), p. 12.

2. I have written about this subject in many books and am actually in the habit of quoting myself. The ideas of genetic engineering and transgenics are very in-teresting. For example, I've often written about pig-lambs, horse-chickens, petunia-cows, and lion-peacocks.

Pythons and Boas

We've all heard about pythons and boa constrictors. We know that they're very dangerous, and in fact, are some of the scariest killers in the snake world. Just what is a python? And how does it differ from a boa?

Unlike other deadly snakes, a python has no venom. Rather, it has enormous power in its body. It wraps itself around a victim and squeezes until the victim stops breathing. In other words, it *constricts* (another word for "squeezes") its prey to death.

A python swallows its victim in one gigantic chunk. The head goes into the snake's mouth first, followed by the rest of the body. The python's jaws are hinged together with stretchy tissues called ligaments, and hence the jaws can open really wide and devour an animal much larger than the snake's mouth. After eating a big animal, such as a monkey, pig, deer, impala, or leopard, a python may pass out from satiation and sleep for weeks.

When I was growing up, my older brother would eat a large Thanksgiving meal and pass out for the rest of the night on the family sofa. I suppose this is the same thing as a python passing out after eating an entire pig, whole. It's just more extreme with the python.

An African Rock Python can grow anywhere from twenty to twenty-eight feet long, and can weigh as much as 200 pounds. Its tongue can smell things. And its upper and lower jaws can sense heat, which is how it finds warm-blooded prey, such as monkeys, pigs, and deer.

So what's a boa constrictor? Like the python, the boa squeezes its prey until the victim can no longer breathe. Then the boa swallows the victim in one gigantic gulp. Boas are nocturnal, which means they hunt at night, and they have been known to eat small crocodilians.

An anaconda is a type of boa and is one of the largest snakes in the world.[3] There have been reports of thirty-seven-foot-long anacondas. This type of snake lives in the swamps of South America.

However, boas are usually smaller in length than pythons. While pythons average twenty feet long, boas may grow to approximately ten feet in length. They average about sixty pounds, which is pretty heavy for a snake but not nearly as heavy as the 200 pounds that a python may carry.

Boas are ovoviviparous, meaning that membranes surround their eggs rather than hard shells. Baby boas just pop through the membrane and crawl into the wild. In other words, baby boas are born "live."

Pythons, on the other hand, are oviparous, which means that their eggs are encased in shells. Python mothers coil their meaty, killer bodies over the shells during in-

---

3. The five largest snakes are the Reticulated Python, Amethystine Python, Anaconda, Indian Python, and African Rock Python.

cubation, and then the baby pythons must crack through the shells—hence, they are not born "live" like baby boas.

Those are the main two differences: size and method of birth.

Both pythons and boas belong to the scientific family called Boidae. The pythons make up twenty-seven species of Boidae, and the boas constitute the other thirty-five species.[4] All pythons and boas have spurs on the bottoms of their tails. The spurs are the remnants of hind legs from prehistoric times. All pythons and boas strike prey and rip through flesh using saw-blade teeth, then they wrap their heavy, powerful coils around the victim and squeeze.

guy is history. The snakes will circle him, then three snakes will lunge and drive venom into the poor guy's cheeks. The guy will fall to the ground, writhing by his campfire (if this is a bad horror movie) or by his four-wheel-drive camper car (if this is a really bad car commercial). Then the snakes will leap on the guy and make goofy faces at him. If that doesn't kill him, then he's a mighty strong man.

Can two snakes drive a car? No. Sorry. But four snakes can drive a bus.

---

4. The numbers vary, depending on the scientist with whom you speak.

How do real "snake traps" work? Some snake traps are just boxes with glue in them. The snake enters the box and sticks to the glue. No kidding.

Other snake traps are made from nets and they hang on fence posts. The snake crawls up the post and gets caught in the net.

Fancier snake traps are wire cages with funnels. The funnels enable snakes to enter, but then the snakes have no way to slither back through the funnels.

By far the most interesting snake trap I know about is the one that uses a smelly mouse. You roast a dead mouse under heat to make it smell really bad. Then you cut off the top of a two-liter soda bottle and stick the dead, smelly mouse into the bottle.

Weirdo Lizards in the World

We've told you about dangerous reptiles and snakes, gigantic lizards, and other oddities. But here, we tell you about some of the more amusing types of weirdo lizards.

Frilled Lizard. When scared, this really strange-looking creature flaps open a huge umbrella-type frill on its head. Then it opens its mouth as widely as it can, and it springs up on its hind legs. If that doesn't work and the predator or scary animal continues to frighten the frilled lizard, it hops away like a bunny, using only its hind legs.

Iguana. These lizard-beasts look as if they are still in prehistoric times. They're long—approximately six or seven feet—and have serrated (that is, saw-tooth) crests down their backs and tails. They also have big flaps of skin under their chins, and the males even have scales beneath their ears.

Gila Monster. This venomous lizard stores fat from ingested food in its tail, and it can live for many months off its tail fat. Only one to two feet long and weighing only three pounds, the Gila is a small lizard, at least when contrasted to an Iguana. But the Gila, as mentioned, is deadly. Its venom is a nerve toxin and, like many snakes, the Gila releases its venom by shooting it down grooved teeth into the victim.

Komodo Dragon. This guy is the world's largest lizard. It can grow to about ten feet and weigh about 300 pounds. It's a fast runner, and it also swims and climbs. It eats large animals, such as deer and goats. And it's also been known to eat men. This grotesque creature has deadly bacteria in its mouth, and after the Dragon bites its prey, the victim dies from blood poisoning induced by the bacteria. *Yuck.* Having wandered off to let the victim die, a few days later, the Dragon will return to the body and eat it.

CHAPTER SIX

Tattoo Me

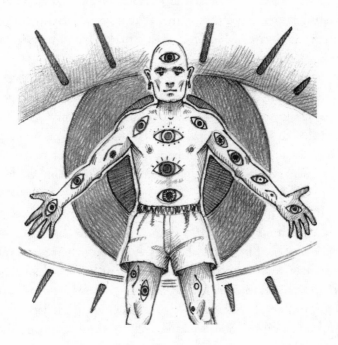

Finally, you have a book that delves into the possible meanings behind Count Olaf's eyeball motif: we'll talk about the eyes in history, from legends to ancient mythology to religion to urban myth. Speaking of eyeballs, is it possible that Count Olaf removed his ankle eyeball tattoo? What is a tattoo, and is it possible to remove it? This chapter will explore all of these subjects, and more.

First, we must address the meaning behind Count Olaf's eyeball tattoo. My guess is that it represents a twisted form of the Evil Eye, which has been a part of human lore for many centuries.

Now, you might think that a person with the Evil Eye is some sort of devilish character, a fiend, a thief, kidnapper, drug dealer to babies—well, someone like Count Olaf. But actually, this is not the case. Rather, the Evil Eye is accidentally cast upon you by somebody who is jealous of you. Jealousy may be a bad thing, but it doesn't quite qualify as pure satanic evil.

If you happen to be Italian, you call the Evil Eye *mal occhio*, which means "the bad eye." And if you're Spanish, you call it *mal ojo*. But this Evil Eye is most everywhere, so if you live in an Arab country, you call it *'ayn*; in Ireland, *droch-shuil*; in Israel, *ayin hara*; in France, *mauvais oeil*; in Germany, *böse Blick*; in Greece, *baskania*; in Haiti, *mauvais jé*; in Holland, *booz blick*; in Norway, *skørtunge*; in Poland, *zte oko*; in Scotland, *bad Ee*; and in Turkey, *nazar*.

Lore about the Evil Eye began in Mesopotamia approximately five thousand years ago. They wrote about the Evil Eye in cuneiform on clay tablets. Some scholars think that people believed in the Evil Eye as long ago as the Upper Paleolithic age. Jews, Christians, and Muslims have all feared the Eye over the course of the centuries. In fact, the people of North Africa, Britain, Scandinavia, India, Spain, Italy, and Portugal all have believed in the Evil Eye.[1]

It is possible (though perhaps not the case) that Count Olaf's ancestors come from Sicily. Or possible (though perhaps not the case) that he has traveled extensively throughout southern Italy and has picked up some ancient customs. For it is only in this part of the world that people believe that a person can deliberately cast the Evil Eye on someone else.

If Violet, Klaus, and Sunny are under the influence of Count Olaf's Evil Eye, there are some ways the orphans can break the curse. Just as various cultures believe in the Evil Eye, they also believe in protective charms and spells that remove the curse.

For example, if a mother thinks that her baby has been placed under the curse of the Evil Eye, she either utters special protective chants or she insults her baby to counteract the "evil" praise that initiated the curse. Sometimes, if a person praises a baby's beauty so much that the mother *fears* the Evil Eye, she smears dirt on the child to make him look ugly,

---

1. If you're seeking clues about an evil Duke, King, or Count's background, it's interesting to note that many cultures and countries have never believed in the Evil Eye. Examples are China, Korea, Thailand, Vietnam, Cambodia, Laos, Taiwan, Indonesia, Japan, Australia, New Zealand, and North American Indians. Of course, this fact may mean absolutely nothing.

hence (in this roundabout logical way) removing the beauty that caused the praise that *could* cause the Evil Eye.

In Pakistan, Iran, and neighboring countries, people who believe in the Evil Eye burn charcoal on the seeds of the aspand plant. They chant protective spells and wave the charcoal smoke toward the child who may be inflicted by the Evil Eye. The charcoal smoke clouds often include burning herbs to give them more power.

So how do you know if your child has the Evil Eye, and how do you cure him? As with everything else, customs vary from culture to culture. The Baudelaire orphans would be wise to try some of these cures, just in case . . .

In Italy, a female orphan who thinks that her brother may be cursed by the Evil Eye drips olive oil into a cup of water. She chants some prayers. She looks into the cup. If all of the olive oil has congealed into one blob that looks like an eyeball, then the brother is cursed by the Evil Eye. For many hours—or for as long as it takes—the sister then utters prayers and drips olive oil into basins of water. When the oil no longer congeals into eyeballs, then her brother is cured.

In Mexico, a mother who thinks her child may be cursed by the Evil Eye puts a chicken egg under the child's bed, then cracks open the shell. If the egg looks like an eye in any way, then the mother assumes that her child has the curse. (My own mother still refuses to eat eggs.)

In Greece, everyone assembles at the local church, and everyone is asked to spit into a cup of holy water. Then the

Protective Charms Against the Evil Eye

I'm not much of an artist, but here are some drawings that show you what various Evil Eye charms look like.

The All-Seeing Eye

This is an eyeball surrounded by beams of light. Ancient Egyptians used the all-seeing eye to represent the protective eye of Horus. It also represents the third eye of Buddha.

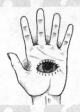

The Eye-in-Hand

This is an eyeball embedded in the palm of a hand. In the eastern Mediterranean, people think of the Evil Eye as blue, and hence, the eye-in-hand charm is also blue.

Horseshoe-and-Eyes

In Europe and North Africa, many people use horseshoes as symbols of good luck. In Turkey, where cultural influ-ences are felt from these other regions, the horseshoe is combined with the eyeball motif to create protective Evil Eye charms.

Eyes-All-Over

Found predominantly in Greece and Turkey, this charm is worn on a necklace. If one blue eye can ward off evil, then a dozen or two of them should really keep you safe.

child must drink the holy water from the cup. In this way, nobody is accused of casting the Evil Eye, yet the child has a chance of being cured. (This explains why all my relatives spit at me during holidays.)

For the ultimate Evil Eye protection, people wear special charms. Most look like eyeballs, though hands and horseshoes are also used. Naturally, there are combinations, such as eyeballs inside hands and eyeballs inside horseshoes. (As you might imagine, my neck is sore from all my eyeball-horseshoe-hands necklaces.)

Some Indian gypsies ward off, or "mirror back," the Evil Eye by wearing extremely ornate mirror charms. Basically, these mirror charms are created by crocheting hundreds of mirrors into wedding cloth or whatever cloth happens to be the fanciest, most expensive kind in the neighborhood.

In parts of Nepal, people wear "the eye of Buddha" to reflect the Evil Eye back onto itself.

The ancient Romans used a "hand of power" to dispel all evil from their homes. Today, Catholics around the world may use a version of the Roman "hand of power" that couples the eyeball motif with the hand. On charms, enormous eyeballs may be embedded in the palms of the crucifixion wounds.

In Israel, Arabia, and India, other forms of "eye-in-hand" charms are used. But always, the image is that of an eyeball in the palm of a hand.

In other parts of the world, people use a blue glass charm to ward off the Evil Eye. Turkish people call their protective charms various names: the all-seeing eye, the horseshoe-and-eyes, or the "eyes-all-over" charm. This last one's pretty cool. It looks like a couple dozen big, blue eyeballs stuck into some clay and worn around the neck.

Also used for protection are eye-agate stones, cat's-eye shells, seeds that look like eyes, and even lemons that resemble eyes.

The ancient Egyptians wore the "eye of Horus" as protection against the Evil Eye. Horus was an Egyptian sky god, and it was believed a charm representing his eyeball would ward off evil.

The son of Egyptian gods Osiris and Isis, Horus had an unusual pair of eyes. His right eye was white, and it shined with the brilliance of the sun. His left eye was black, and it glowered with the darkness of the overcast moon. Horus had an evil brother, Seth, who killed their father, Osiris. If that weren't enough evil, Seth then ripped out his brother Horus' left eyeball. But all was not lost, for Horus won his battle against Seth, and then magically, the moon somehow teamed up with the god of writing—a guy named Thoth—and restored Horus' eyeball.

The Eye of Horus amulet consisted of precisely measured eyeball parts. Exactly one sixty-fourth of the eyeball is missing from the amulet and represents the dash of magic added by Thoth. In ancient Egypt, the Eye of Horus amulet protected the dead from evil, and the amulet was placed on mummies, tombs, and coffins.

Another protection against the Evil Eye has to do with

Medusa from Greek mythology. Do you remember the story of Medusa? She was the one whose hair was made of writhing snakes and whose stare could turn a guy into a block of stone.

Well, by now, you're thinking something like, "Medusa . . . stare turns a guy into a block of stone . . . Evil Eye . . . stare kills people. Did Medusa have the Evil Eye?" If you are thinking something like this, then you're pretty smart and you cobble (which just means assemble) ideas together very quickly. If, on the other hand, you sat there thinking something like, "Medusa . . . stare turns a guy into a block of stone. . . . Evil Eye . . . stare kills people. I don't get it," then what can I say?

But back to Medusa and the Evil Eye. Medusa was one of the three Gorgon sisters.[2] Like Medusa, Stheno and Euryale also had snake hair, and all three girls were so incredibly ugly that a single glance from one of them would kill you. Specifically, you'd turn into stone.

The interesting part of all this is that Medusa's head is viewed as both the ultimate Evil Eye and also the cure for the Evil Eye. Why? According to Greek mythology, Athena gave Perseus her shield to reflect Medusa's image back at her. Athena figured that the shield would thus protect Perseus

---

2. Not to be confused with the Pointer sisters, Destiny's Child, or Britney Spears.

from Medusa's Evil Eye. So if you wear an amulet that looks like Medusa's head, you are protected from the Evil Eye of neighbors, witches, rival tribesmen, unscrupulous salesmen (meaning "having no morals whatsoever, would sell you a school cafeteria lunch for a hundred bucks, claiming it's caviar from the south of France"), your mean Uncle Horus, and the principal.

Trying to track down Count Olaf by finding out who gave him the tattoo would be an impossible task. It's been estimated that forty-two million people, or more, in North America alone have tattoos. And all over the world, the tattoo is very popular as well. Almost every language has a word that means "tattoo." Examples are *Tätowier, tatoveringer, tatuaggio, tatuar, tatoeage, tattueringar, tatuagens, tatouage,* and *tatuaje.* A hundred years ago, sailors wore tattoos to protect themselves from drowning. In some cultures, tattoos are created over the heart in hopes of stopping bullets from killing people.

A tattoo, of course, is an ink drawing on somebody's skin. I happen to be terrified of needles, even for drawing blood or giving flu shots; so for me, tattoos are totally out of the question. However, for somebody like Count Olaf, tattoos are well worth the pain.

Possibly (though unlikely because I am a total liar), Count Olaf went to a guy in a shop guarded by pit bulls and rottweilers. This shop was probably in the worst part of the worst town. The tattoo machine was probably built in 1902.

The tattoo machine was probably never cleaned and had grime from a thousand men smeared all over it. Like a sewing machine for flesh, the tattoo machine probably drilled its needle into Count Olaf's ankle, over and over, as quickly as you can imagine, straight through the outer layer of skin (epidermis) and into the middle layer of the skin (dermis). It deposited ink into the dermis.

After obtaining the eyeball tattoo, the Count probably had to wipe all oozing fluids from his ankle every fifteen minutes. He had to apply antibacterial ointments to the tattoo. And he had to cease his most favorite activities: Jacuzzis, hot tubs, tanning salons, football. He could not shave his ankle. He could not blow his nose on it. (He asked me to do it, but I refused.) He could not scratch or pick at it, and he could not rub his tattoo all over an alley cat or the shop owner's pit bull. Of course, you can believe this or not, but if you think that I'm making it all up, then one of us is a total loser.

Now let's suppose that the Count wants to remove his tattoo. It's pretty difficult to completely remove a tattoo from the skin. After all, the ink is deposited into the middle layer of the skin, not on the skin's surface.

However, there are some ways that the Count could remove his tattoo. The most modern method is to use lasers, which stands for "Light Amplification by the Stimulated Emission of Radiation." Three types of lasers are currently used to remove tattoos. One is called the Q-switched Ruby, another the Q-switched Alexandrite, and the third is known as the Q-switched Nd: YAG. The Nd: YAG type is very good at removing black, red, and blue ink from the skin.[3]

The lasers shoot short light pulses into the skin, where the tattoo ink absorbs the light. The tattoo ink then splinters into tiny pieces. The body's immune system takes over and removes the tiny pieces.

---

3. The hardest tattoo colors to remove are yellow and green.

CHAPTER SEVEN

Fancy-Pants Words

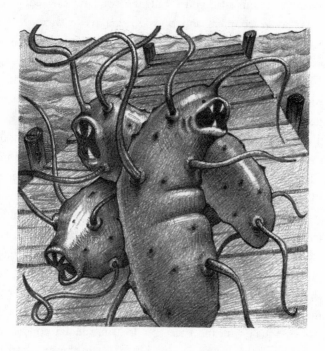

The Lemony Snicket books are packed with sophisticated vocabulary words and their meanings. This chapter will touch on interesting words in the Snicket books, and will also give you some new words to ponder. I'll supply a personal list of cool words, culled from my (pathetic) childhood obsession with my thesaurus. One example: absquatulate—what a great word! It should be used all the time! Other favorites are oxymoron and funambulist. How are unusual words used in the Lemony Snicket books and in real life?

Isadora, as I'm sure you recall, is always writing couplets. Just what *are* couplets and how do you write them? We'll concoct a few amusing couplets using some of the "fancy" words in the Snicket books.

So let's get started. First of all, what's a *quagmire?* This is a good place to start, since Duncan and Isadora's last name happens to be Quagmire.

I've always thought of a quagmire as a muddy, complex place. It could be a real pit of quicksand, for example, or just the feeling that your miserable life with all its problems is so muddy and complex that you feel as if you're living in a pit of quicksand. Whether it's literally a sooty, sandy, or muddy place or just a depressing place in your head, a quagmire is a precarious place to be. I wouldn't want to be Duncan Quagmire—dunk in quagmire, what a name!

And what about Esmé Squalor? Sure, she has a cool name, but does *squalor* mean something horrible?[1] Of course, it does. Squalor means that you live in squalid conditions. Squalid means that you live in filthy circumstances. For example, your home could be a dump, falling to pieces and filled with debris, garbage, slime, mold, mildew, dust, and rotting food. Or your home could be a place of great shame, a

---

1. We can assume that most everything in a Lemony Snicket book has a horrible meaning, right?

sordid place where only filthy, rotten people hang out. The ultimate in squalor would be living with filthy, rotten people in a dump that's falling to pieces and filled with debris, garbage, slime, mold, mildew, dust, and rotting food.

With squalor behind us, let's look at some more interesting words I compiled from the Lemony Snicket books. Snicket is brilliant at inserting fancy words into his books. I am not so brilliant. The best I can do is arrange some of the words alphabetically, then tell you what they mean. I will also stick some of my own words into the list, just to keep you on your toes. This way, you'll have to guess which words are from Snicket and which words are from Lois. (But don't worry, I always give you the answers anyway.)

An **abomination** is something that is extremely disgusting and loathsome. For example, the tin shack with the crabs where the Baudelaire orphans are forced to live is an abomination. You could say that Count Olaf is an abominable man. (If you won't say it, then I'll say it for you, because Count Olaf *is* an abominable man.) And now you know what the abominable snowman is: a snowman who is disgusting and loathsome. This word, abomination, seemed like the perfect word to kick off our list of interesting Snicket-type words. It sums up the lives of the Baudelaire orphans pretty well.

Absquatulate. This word is not in my dictionary. But my mother used it on me, and when I asked her for the meaning, she replied, "Absquatulate means 'hie.'" So I thought, hmm, can I slap someone's palm and instead of saying, "High five," can I say, "Absquatulate five"? I'm sorry to tell you that the answer is no. *Hie* does not mean "high." Hie, which *is* in my dictionary, means "hurry."

Adversity is what the Baudelaire orphans face throughout all their adventures. In Book the Fifth, *The Austere Academy*, Lemony Snicket describes the word as meaning "Count Olaf."[2] And that's pretty funny. What adversity really means, of course, is a condition of extreme suffering and misfortune. Sadly, that definition only begins to describe the conditions under which the orphans live.

An **alcove** is a very small nook.[3] This nook can be in a garden, forest, living room, bedroom, bathroom, kitchen, cave, or underground pool of water: it can be anywhere. It can be on the moon. We get this English word from the French *al-côve*, which comes from the Spanish *alcoba*, which comes from the Arabic *al-qubba*, which means "the vault." So long ago in Arabia, some guy may have put his jewels and daggers into al-qubba, or into the vault. Perhaps they had very large vaults in Arabia; perhaps they had vaults the size of very small nooks.

Anagrams are words or phrases that have exactly the same letters in them. Anagrams are key to Klaus's detective work in

---

2. Book the Fifth, *The Austere Academy,* p. 20.

3. While a reference is made to an alcove in Book the Second, *The Reptile Room,* p. 34, I supply a longer definition for you here. Sometimes, it's fun to delve into where these words come from; in this case, the word *alcove* comes from the Arabic word *al-qubba,* which means "the vault."

Book the Eighth, *The Hostile Hospital*. For example, he notes that Violet Baudelaire and Albert E. Deviloeia are not quite anagrams. How do they differ? Look closely. For each letter in Violet Baudelaire, put a mark over the same letter that appears in Albert E. Deviloeia. Violet's name has a "u" that is not in Albert's name. And Albert's name has an extra "e" that is not in Violet's name. So they are not quite anagrams.

Now I know that one of your favorite Lemony Snicket words is probably **aphorism**. Well, if it isn't one of your favorite words, it should be. It sure beats words like *nostrils* and *school*. Lemony's definition is the best, of course,[4] though I wouldn't mind hearing Sunny's use of the word aphorism.

Sometimes, I laugh so much when thinking about Sunny that it gets me in trouble. For example, once I was in a very serious business meeting with two customers, my two bosses, and a cannonball. The customers and bosses were talking about some work they wanted me to do. I heard fragments of the conversation, such as "Overtime? Eighty hours a week? Sure, no problem," and, "Lois will reprogram your 12,574 Web pages within a month." I began to doze off, which is always a mistake when I'm summoned to a meeting in the cannonball room. I thought of Sunny. Schmeek Coik! Galfuskin! Prem! I jolted awake, laughing hysterically. The big boss was priming the cannonball, which was pointed at my nose. "What did you say?" she screamed. The smell of

---

4. Book the Seventh, *The Vile Village*, p. 13.

burned charcoal filled my nostrils for a moment, then *kerbam!*, the boss taught me a huge lesson. Never fall asleep, never think about Sunny, and never laugh when you're in a cannon-ball room meeting. What had I said? What had I done? Well, apparently, when asked if I would reprogram the 12,574 Web pages within a month, I shrieked in Sunny style: "Schmeek! Vazgluskin condemno your wife and chil-dreno forevero! Workphobia workphobia glark snarf glark!" Needless to say, I am no longer working there.

But we were talking about aphorisms, weren't we? See how my mind strays? This is why I am not a high-level cor-porate executive or lawyer. This is why I am a goofy writer. Oh. Aphorisms. I take it that you *really* have to know the definition of an aphorism, else you wouldn't be pounding on me like this to tell you. All right, then.

An aphorism is a brief statement of truth or opinion that people somewhat believe because it has been stated for so long. Here's an example: Good things come in small pack-ages. This is an aphorism; it is a brief statement of opinion that has been accepted as truth due to its long use. A dis-tasteful aphorism is: Children should be seen and not heard. Here's another one: People who live in glass houses shouldn't throw stones.

Blanched green beans are briefly boiled green beans.[5] This is true, but there are other definitions of the word blanched.

---

5. Book the First, *The Bad Beginning,* p. 13.

For example, blanch can also mean "take the color out of, or bleach." When he heard that he'd be working at the Piffle-rock School for Juvenile Mercenaries, Joey's entire body blanched. This doesn't mean that his body was boiled alive, but, rather, that all of his skin went totally white.

Blurp. Sunny might use this word when trying to say, "Where is the kitchen? I need some cookies."[6] I generally say something similar to "blurp" when I've eaten too many cookies.

Bromidrosiphobia means "fear of body odor." I suppose this phobia means that you're terrified of either smelling somebody who isn't wearing deodorant or smelling bad your-self. If you're afraid of smelling somebody else who hasn't washed for a long time, then it would be very hard for you to go anywhere in public. Because there's always *somebody* who smells bad, right? Usually, this smelly person is squeezed into a bus or subway seat next to you for several hours. Though you never know: you could be minding your own business, humming, and walking down the street, and a hideously mal-odorous (meaning "smelly") guy could come out of nowhere, slam into you, knock you to the ground, and fall on top of you. He smells like a latrine, his breath is like roadkill. Not good if you have bromidrosiphobia. Hey, that wouldn't be so great if you *don't* have bromidrosiphobia. One final point I will make is, if you have bromidrosiphobia, you probably

---

6. I made up this one. Sunny does not say "blurp."

aren't going to do very well in gym class. And if you're afraid of being afraid, then you have a condition known as phobophobia.

Callous. This adjective means "emotionally hardened and unfeeling." Here's an example: By the time he was four years old, Johnny had lived with 104 different legal guardians. When his 105th legal guardian showed up to take him "home," Johnny glared at him and shrugged. Mr. Moe Misery didn't stand a chance. Years of neglect had left Johnny callous. There's also a verb callous, which means "to make or become callous."

Callus. This noun means that you have hardened skin on your elbow, toe, or thumb, as in "I have a callus on my big toe." The verb callus means "to form hardened tissue." Because he had calluses on 99 percent of his body, he was calloused to the thought of warts.

Cucumbers are on Aunt Josephine's grocery list.[7] When the Baudelaires first arrive at her house, Aunt Josephine serves chilled cucumber soup. Now that's all fine and nice, but you're probably wondering why I put cucumbers on this list of interesting words. After all, how interesting can the word cucumber be?

I have a very good reason for putting cucumbers on my list. You see, it's unknown to me (and hence, causing me great anxiety) what *kind* of cucumbers are on Aunt Josephine's gro-

---

7. Book the Third, *The Wide Window*, p. 87.

cery list. This is not as simple a matter as you might think. For example, there are sea cucumbers, horned cucumbers, bur cucumbers, and squirting cucumbers.

If Aunt Josephine wants sea cucumbers, then she intends to procure (which means "buy") echinoderms that have tentacles around their mouths. Eh, what? Cucumbers with tentacles and mouths? Just what is Lois babbling about this time? Well, I'll tell you. An echinoderm is a marine animal that has symmetrical parts, such as a starfish or a sea cucumber. This is why the sea cucumber has tentacles and a mouth: because it is an animal. So if Aunt Josephine wants to buy sea cucumbers, she will have to go to an aquarium, to the wharf, or out to sea on a giant fishing vessel. And then, who knows how she'll cook the things? I've never eaten sea cucumbers. Maybe you make fancy little sandwiches with them. Maybe you make soufflés out of them. Maybe you make puddings, cakes, or pies out of them. Rather than lemon meringue pie, you could make a lemon sea cucumber pie, for example. Or for your birthday, have a sea cucumber cake.

If Aunt Josephine is after horned cucumbers, then she'll be purchasing an African tropical plant that has oblong, spiny, orange-red fruits. In this case, I suppose she'll have to go to Africa to procure her cucumbers. Upon return, she might ditch the applesauce and use horned cucumber sauce instead.

If she's feeling threatened and wants to protect herself (which is very likely), she might intend to buy squirting cucumbers. These are hairy Mediterranean vines with exploding fruits. When the cucumber fruits are ripe, they shoot their seeds and juice like bullets. You know this could be useful if you live in a dangerous city. Get a few squirting cucumbers, and when some creeps try to rob you, knock you down, beat you up, or blow you to smithereens, all you have to do is pull out a squirting cucumber and let 'em have it!

Demise is a fancy word for total ruin or "death." The Baudelaires are constantly in threat of their demise. I had to include this word because it is something I worry about whenever I read a Lemony Snicket book. I fear for Sunny's demise. And then there was the time the Count whacked Klaus, and I feared for Klaus's demise. I figure Violet can handle herself pretty well, for she can always invent something to prevent her demise.

Despair. This is another excellent Baudelaire word, isn't it? It means "complete loss of hope." I needn't say anything more.

Deus ex machina usually means that an author has put a gun in a book just because the hero happens to need a gun at that moment. Another way of explaining this Latin phrase is to say that something very helpful comes along when it is totally unexpected. For example, suppose a terrorist is dangling you from a cliff by your two little toes, and he tells you that he'll pull you up and set you free, if and only if you give him a copy of this book. So you pull this very book from beneath your pants belt (where it's been held securely inside your pants as you've been hanging upside down, squirming and begging for your life), and you thrust it at the terrorist. "Aha," he cries, "the very book I've been dying to read for

more than a year now! I shall set you free, my lad (or lassy)!"
And violà, he yanks you up, and then you go running for
your life, missing this excellent book but retaining your miserable existence. The book has functioned as your deus ex
machina.

Or let's say there's an adventure story, in which the hero
needs one screw to save the entire world. This particular
screw, however, is only made in Malaysia once every decade,
and then they only make two such screws. The hero is
nowhere near Malaysia. Rather, he's lost on the polar ice cap.
But he needs that screw, and violà, suddenly a polar bear
wanders by and a rare Malaysian screw drops from its mouth.
Deus ex machina.[8]

Disconsolate. If you're disconsolate, you're so dejected and
sad that nothing can cheer you up. This word means
"gloomy," so it's safe to say that the Baudelaires live in disconsolate surroundings all the time and it's amazing that
they're not thoroughly disconsolate themselves.

An **ermine** is a weasel with white winter fur. Generally, if
someone calls you a weasel, you've been insulted. It implies
that you're a slimy, lying, unsympathetic moron. Of interest
is the fact that the word ermine has a meaning beyond
weasel. If someone has an executive office or a role in gov-

---

8. The concept of deus ex machina is discussed in Book the Seventh, *The Vile
Village*, p. 177. However, I supplied all of the definitions and silly examples given
in this book.

ernment that requires that he wears a robe adorned with ermine fur, then that person is called an ermine. So if he's chairman of the school district and he must wear a special jacket with an ermine collar during school award ceremonies and parades, then he could be known as an ermine, or basically, a weasel. Don't ever tell anyone that I told you about this one. Let it be our secret.

According to Klaus, **fata morgana** is a mirage, whereby you think you see something that isn't really there.[9] Yes, this is a mirage, whereby you generally think you see a body of water, such as a lake in the middle of the desert. A fata morgana is caused when layers of hot and cold air distort the light.

Feigning means "pretending to be something you're not." For example, when Count Olaf is a detective, he's feigning that he's a law-abiding person, when in actuality he's a murderer. You can feign another person's voice. You can feign sleep.

Although the word sounds as if you're extremely patriotic and display many flags on your house, car, horse, donkey, and clothing, **flagitiousness** actually means "wicked, vicious, brutal criminal activity." Once again, I'm reminded of Count Olaf.

A **funambulist** is someone who walks on ropes. This doesn't sound like much fun to me.

Mr. Poe purchases clothing of **grotesque** colors for the

---

9. Book the Seventh, *The Vile Village*, p. 24.

Baudelaire orphans.[10] This means that their clothes have ludicrous colors in them or colors that simply don't match. An outfit of grotesque colors might be: orange-and-purple-plaid shirt with green velvet sleeves; puke yellow vinyl pants; neon pink feather boa.

An **idiosyncracy** is an odd habit that makes you appear somewhat eccentric to other people.[11] I probably have many idiosyncracies. One odd habit I have is that I write goofy books. Another idiosyncracy is that I read comic books (I remind you that I am an adult). I enjoy watching birds with my cat every morning. I think they're beautiful, and she's just hungry, but, still, most people do not watch birds every morning with their cat.

Insipid means "dim-witted, lacking attributes that cause excitement, interest, or stimulation." (An attribute is a factor.) Here's a typical day in my life: I awaken, drooling on my pillow. I lift the cat off the back of my skull. In my pajamas, I go downstairs, with the cat bouncing ahead of me. I stand by the back window. I stoop and lift the cat. Together, we watch the birds for an hour. I sit at my computer and write this chapter about words. I belch a few times. I may scratch my belly two dozen times. I talk to nobody all day. I do talk to the cat, however, mainly to comment about especially chubby blue jays. I drink soup. I climb into bed. I

---

10. Book the First, *The Bad Beginning*, p. 13.
11. Book the Sixth, *The Ersatz Elevator*, p. 123.

watch Mr. Ed. I fall asleep. The cat climbs onto my head and settles in for the night. Do I lead an insipid life?[12]

Malevolence means "wishing harm to others and having evil intentions." Who is filled with malevolence? Violet? No. Sunny? No. Lois? No. Count Olaf? *Maybe* . . .

According to both my dictionary and thesaurus, a **misnomer** is "a wrong name."[13] Uncle Monty, who defines the term in a nearly identical way, probably had the same dictionary and thesaurus that my mother bought for me.[14] Let's suppose you have a "working mother." This phrase implies that a lot of mothers are lazy bums who never do any work at all. After all, if your mother is a "working mother" but your friend Tom's mother is not a "working mother," then what does Tom's mother do all day? Do we assume that Tom's mother is a sloth, who never gets out of bed, who maybe eats ice cream all day while she watches Mr. Ed on television? The word "mother" implies that somebody is working extremely hard, if only to raise her children, clean the house, buy the food, cook the

---

12. The answer is no. Are you surprised? In my life, there are two beings: me and the cat. To the cat, I am a hotbed of wild excitement, sharing all of her interests. And in my life, who else matters? So therefore, my life is fascinating and anything but insipid.

13. My dictionary is a standard-issue Webster's that dates back to when I was in fourth grade. The standard-issue Roget's Thesaurus is its fourth-grade counterpart. I doubt that the word *misnomer* has changed much since I was a kid, some 150 years ago.

14. Book the Second, *The Reptile Room*, p. 29.

meals, wash the laundry, chop the wood, mow the lawn, feed the goats, shampoo the hens, and nag you fourteen hours a day. So the term "working mother" is a misnomer.

Another misnomer is "stained glass." Most colored glass is not stained. By the sixteenth century, stained glass was created by using enamel paints.

To **mollify** someone is to calm him down.[15] After my cat Chantel tried unsuccessfully to catch and eat a bird, I mollified her by crooning her name and petting her fur. When I came home from work with cannonball charcoal on my face, Chantel mollified me by squeaking and rubbing her fur against the back of my skull.

A **monocle** is one lens in a pair of eyeglasses. For example, the cannonball blew out my right eye. So I am missing my right eye (which had perfect 20/20 vision), while my left eye is near-sighted in one-quarter, far-sighted in one-third, and lopsided everywhere else. I now wear a monocle over my left eye. And I stumble around, banging into walls and cursing.

Mortification means "shame and wounded pride, humiliation." After they hit me with the cannonball and fired me from the job, I was filled with mortification. With my one eyeball, the lopsided left one, and no monocle yet to help me see, I slithered on my belly like a snake all the way home— 132 miles I slithered—weeping in shame during the whole

---

15. Book the Third, *The Wide Window*, p. 145.

journey. If you are caught reading this dreadful book, you will be mortified.

Nefarious.[16] Ooh, a very good word, indeed. Evil, evil, evil: that's what nefarious means. Some synonyms for nefarious are abominable (remember that word?), contemptible, despicable, disgusting, foul, lousy, odious, rotten, and vile. Using your lowest voice, deep and dark, say the word nefarious very slowly . . . ne . . . far . . . i . . . ous. A chill should go down your back. Better yet, point your finger at the most nefarious bully in your school and shriek, "Nefarious bully!" Now run for your life.

Obdurate. Hard-hearted and wicked, an obdurate monster inflicts pain and abuse upon those around him. Mr. Scrooge is an obdurate miser.

Oxymoron. When conflicting terms are put together, they form an oxymoron. For example, "deafening silence" is an oxymoron because silence cannot be deafening; that is, you don't hear anything in silence, so how can you be deafened by no sound? The term *oxy* comes from a Greek word meaning "sharp"; and the term *moron* means "foolish and dull." So you have oxy/sharp plus moron/dull, and a sharp dull-witted moron makes no sense. So the word oxymoron itself is an oxy-

---

16. This is a creepy-sounding word that is used several times in the Lemony Snicket books. I have used this word for decades, so I'm including it in the list of cool words.

moron. I bet your teacher doesn't even know that oxymoron
is an oxymoron.

Phlegm. All of that intelligent supposition (meaning "pondering") about oxymorons has left my brain in a state of soggy mush.
Therefore, I am capable at this moment only of giving you the
word phlegm. This is the mucus secreted by your respiratory
tract when you have a cold or the flu. You cough up phlegm.

[Lois is now pausing before her brain can move from
phlegm back into more intellectual realms. Chantel is on the
back of Lois's skull. Lois is drooling onto her pillow. Mr. Ed
is on the television.]

[Thirty minutes have passed.]

Okay, I'm back. I bet you were afraid that I wasn't going
to finish writing this book for you. Sometimes, I need to rest
my brain, but I always come back and move to the next word.
Which in this case is . . .

Quandary, meaning you are in a predicament, and you don't
know what to do. A predicament means that something difficult or disturbing has occurred, and you must decide how to
resolve the problem.[17] A few minutes ago, I was in a quandary.
I was drooling onto my pillow with a gigantic cat on my head.[18]

---

17. The word is used in Book the Seventh, *The Vile Village*, p. 123. However, I
made up the definition.

18. Chantel weighs fifteen pounds and has extremely long fur. She also has a fair
amount of flubber.

I knew that I had to pull myself off that bed and return to my office and finish this chapter. But my brain was soggy mush. I could not think. I could not move. I could only drool and listen to the talking horse. So I was in a quandary. If I didn't get up and finish this chapter, all would be lost! My publisher would cancel my contract, and hence my life would be in ruins. Luckily, I was able to snap out of it and . . .

relinquish myself to the harsh reality of adult work. This means that I gave myself up to what must be done. I relinquished or surrendered myself to the task at hand.

With **revulsion,**[19] I wiped the drool from my cheeks. I rose from that bed. I marched into this office. I ate fourteen pounds of chocolate. I ate twelve hundred peanuts. I am now rooted—literally rooted—to this chair, unable to move. And I will finish this chapter for you, my faithful readers.

Salmonella. This is a rod-shaped bacteria that causes food poisoning and typhoid. It was named after the American pathologist Daniel Elmer Salmon. A pathologist studies diseases. I was very sly in this paragraph and slipped in two new words for you rather than one. And now, I will provide absolutely no transition from salmonella to our next word, skittish.

A **segue** (pronounced seg-way) is a transition in conversation or in written material.[20]

---

19. Book the First, *The Bad Beginning,* p. 50.
20. Book the Second, *The Reptile Room,* p. 36.

I refuse to give you a segue.

Skittish means nervous, as in "all Baudelaire relatives are skittish about helping the orphans because they fear Count Olaf."[21]

[No segue for you—such power I feel!]

Standoffish means antisocial.[22] Because I work here, all alone, writing this book, perhaps I am perceived as being a standoffish person. Actually, I'm a sitoften person. I wonder why we don't have a word, crouchoffish, for people who have standophobia, or the fear of standing.[23]

Unnerving means "upsetting." It was unnerving to see Phil's mangled leg.[24]

That's it, folks. I'm beginning to feel unnerved by writing this chapter. Clearly, I am capable of no more.

However, I have sufficient energy to tell you about couplets for a few minutes. Isadora writes couplets as clues in the Lemony Snicket books. I figure it might be fun to merge some of our fancy words with the notion of couplets. You can even try this at home.

A couplet is a poem that is two lines long. The ends of

---

21. Book the Seventh, *The Vile Village.*

22. Book the First, *The Bad Beginning,* p. 74.

23. I just invented the word standophobia. But I bet there are people with a fear of standing, as well as people with a fear of crouching and sitting. There are even people who fear string beans. I kid you not. That particular fear is called linonophobia.

24. Book the Fourth, *The Miserable Mill,* p. 97.

both lines rhyme with each other. You might want to write a few couplets using the words from this chapter. It's rather fun, as in:

His linonophobia was quite acute
He shrieked in horror at the string in his soup

My nefarious parent worked me like a slave
He was a weasel who didn't behave

Deus ex machina, bam went the gun
It shouldn't have been there, logic was none

Do not your happiness feign
Else your life will be in vain

Mr. Ed is my favorite guy
He is the only horse who does not lie

CHAPTER EIGHT

Marital Law: Can an Old Geezer Marry a Young Girl?

In the first book, Count Olaf manipulates events every way he can to try and marry fourteen-year-old Violet. He makes her perform in a play, hoping to marry her without her knowledge. The marriage is to happen as part of the theatrical performance, yet be a valid and very real wedding. Basically, he wants to control the Baudelaire fortune, which will be hers when she is all grown up. As her husband, he assumes that he can access the entire Baudelaire inheritance, spend it as he wants, and leave nothing for the three orphans.

Nice guy, eh?

In this chapter, we'll explore the harsh realities behind Count Olaf's marriage plans. For example, is it legal for a grown man to marry a fourteen-year-old girl? If a man is a girl's legal guardian acting in loco parentis ("in the place of a parent"), is it legal for him to become her husband?

And to lighten things up, I'll tell you about some weird and famous marriages that happened in real life. You'll learn, for example, about a guy who was married twenty-nine times.

First let's take a look at how young you're allowed to be when you get married. Can you be fourteen years old?

In the United States, marriage is regulated by each state. The Supreme Court has given this right to the states. All states do take into consideration matters such as the ages of and the relationship between the man and woman. My interpretation of this is that a nine-year-old girl cannot marry an eighty-year-old man. A legal guardian cannot marry his "daughter."

In Alabama, you can get married at age fourteen. You need the consent of your parent or legal guardian, which in Violet's case would be Count Olaf himself.

According to a Georgia newspaper,[1] a sixteen-year-old can

---

1. See www.onlineathens.com/stories/052301/opi0523010014.shtml. The article appeared in the *Athens Banner-Herald* on Wednesday, May 23, 2001.

get married in that state, but, again, only if she has parental consent. The newspaper article also points out that a child can marry at fourteen in Arkansas, and in Mississippi, at any age with parental consent.

Many states allow marriages of girls of any age if the girls are expecting babies. For example, an expectant teenage girl in Delaware, Florida, Georgia, Kentucky, Maryland, or Oklahoma can get married without her parents' permission. And if the girl already has a baby, she can marry the father. The only hitch here is that poor Violet would have to be expecting a child with the disgusting and hideous Count Olaf for him to get away with marriage. And this situation is highly unlikely.

In Florida, the Count might be able to get away with it. If the bride is under the age of sixteen, a county judge must issue a marriage license.[2]

The key factor in all of this is that the Count is Violet's legal guardian. As such, would a court really allow him to sign the papers required for him to marry the underage Violet? *Absolutely not.*

If dragged into Arkansas, Tennessee, or Mississippi, Violet could find herself married to the Count even at the age of fourteen. However, I do not believe that a young girl can be forced into marriage to her legal guardian anywhere in the United States.

---

2. See www.teenmarriagelaws.com.

In other countries, girls can also get married at very young ages.[3] For example, Harvard University reports that the average marital age of girls in Asian Uttar Pradesh is fourteen. In Rajastan, it is most common for women to marry at thirteen and fourteen years of age. And in Madhya Pradesh, the average age for girls to marry is at fourteen and fifteen years of age. So perhaps the Count can drag poor Violet to Rajastan or Madhya Pradesh, and then marry her.

Now, certain mail-order ministries can perform marriages, and generally, states do not interfere with religious matters. It's a real stretch to imagine that such a marriage would be considered legal, but if the Count gets a mail-order ministry type of marriage, then he might possibly be considered Violet's husband.

On the other hand, for a marriage to be valid, both wife and husband must voluntarily consent to the wedding. If a girl gives consent to marriage, but she feels forced to do so for any reason, then the marriage is invalid. For example, if you fear for the lives of your siblings and get married to save their necks, then the marriage is invalid. If an evil Count is threatening you in any way, then the marriage is invalid. Any way you dice it, Violet isn't going to consent to a wedding with Count Olaf.

Also on Violet's side is the fact that a marriage is consid-

---

3. This data is culled from a Harvard University study at www.hsph.harvard.edu/grhfasia/forums/Tribals/Tribals/MT003.HTM.

ered "void"—that is, totally worthless—if it violates some basic moral principle, such as "old-guy legal guardian forcing his 'daughter' to marry him."

In the case of any type of invalid or void marriage, Violet can obtain an annulment from the court. An annulment means that the marriage essentially never even took place.

Throughout history, parents have arranged marriages for their children. At the time of birth, a girl might be betrothed (or promised in marriage to) an infant boy, a teenaged guy, or even a guy her parents' age. Princes and kings often married just to produce male heirs to the throne. Men would have many wives, and all wives would produce children. In ancient Rome, parents arranged marriages for their children to appease or to simply please ancestral spirits. In ancient Greece, parents arranged marriages for their children, as well, in this case mainly to protect innocent young girls and to produce as many grandchildren as possible. For more information, see "Marital Law in Ancient Rome" (pages 105–107) and "Marital Law in Ancient Greece" (pages 107–108).

Throughout history, of course, people have married to improve their social status or increase their wealth. Older people who are lonely may get married for companionship. The best reason to get married, of course, is because you love somebody.

Clearly, the Count does not love Violet. He just wants her money.

If somehow forced into a valid marriage with this creep, Violet could have him thrown in jail for child abuse. After all, he is her legal guardian. Basically, if a child is under eighteen years of age and is subjected to physical abuse (including marrying an old guy and the kind of punishment and beatings the Count inflicts on the orphans), then that child is essentially a victim of abuse. If Violet can prove that Count Olaf is abusive, then all of the orphans can be rid of him. Of course, Count Olaf is literally getting away with murder, so pinning him with child abuse probably wouldn't work.

I don't know about you, but my head hurts from thinking about this subject. I think we need to end this chapter on a much lighter note.

For example, let's consider some wacky marriages and crazy statistics.

According to a newspaper in England last year,[4] officials discovered that between them, two sisters had married twenty-four men. The "sham" weddings (which means bogus or "not exactly on the up and up") were performed so the men could legally enter England, hence bypassing any stringent immigration laws that might keep them out of the country.

The newspaper further reported that the sisters were paid handsomely for getting married. The average amount per marriage was 1,500 pounds, or $2,537.88; though in lieu of money, the sisters accepted furniture, such as chairs, tables, and garbage cans.

---

4. Paul Eastham, *Cutting Daily Mail*, April 2, 2002, as reported at www.walkwales.org.uk/weddings.htm.

Marital Law in Ancient Rome

In ancient Rome, the word for marriage was *matrimonium*. The root, or base part, of matrimonium was *mater*, which means "mother." Today, we have another word for marriage: matrimony; and it refers to the same thing, the union of two people so that one of them (the female, of course) can become a mother.

The ancient Romans actually had no governmental jurisdiction or authority over marriages. This means that people could get married without a government marriage license or judge. However, the law stated that people had to have "the right to get married," which the Romans called connubium. If Count Olaf lived in ancient Rome, he would probably finagle (which means "figure out in a sly manner") a way to obtain the connubium to marry Violet Baudelaire.

To have connubium, both girl and boy had to be either a patrician or a plebeian. A patrician was born to a noble family, with exclusive rights to be a Senator. A plebeian, on the other hand, was an ordinary person with no rights whatsoever to be a Senator. In addition, both boy and girl had to obtain the consent of their families. A girl had to be twelve years old, a boy had to be fourteen. So if Count Olaf and fourteen-year-old Violet were both plebeians, for example, and both obtained the consent of their families, they could have married in ancient Rome.

Of particular interest to those of us who wonder about Count and Mrs. Violet Olaf . . .

. . . and I cringe even to write the above phrase . . . was that if a wife died, the husband could keep one-fifth of her dowry for each child the two of them had together. The rest of the deceased wife's dowry would return to her family—for example, to Klaus and Sunny. In Count and Mrs. Olaf's case, Violet's death would serve no real financial purpose to the Count, so he'd be better off keeping her alive and just stealing her money every day.

Now in ancient Rome, there were two types of marriage, in manum and not in manum. In either case, the Count would be very well off by marrying the fourteen-year-old Violet. Back then, a marriage in manum gave all of the wife's property to the husband. She basically became equivalent to his daughter. (Weird, but true.) No doubt, Count Olaf would seek a marriage in manum to Violet Baudelaire. Why? Because a marriage not in manum allowed the wife's family to maintain control of her fortune.

Of course, as with all other things in life, there were loopholes to the in manum marriage. Given Violet's intelligence, she would have learned about these loopholes and used them, hence foiling the Count's plans to steal the orphans' inheritance.

For example, if a wife stayed away from her husband

for three nights during the first year of marriage, her worldly possessions might not fall to her husband. I'm sure a battle ensued, and most likely, the husband won the money anyway, but, at least, a wretched twelve-year-old bride might have *some* chance of escape.

In ancient Rome, there were even marriage arrangements for slaves (called contuberium), and for marriages between slaves and freemen (called concubinatus).

Marital Law in Ancient Greece

In ancient Greece, a girl usually got married at age fourteen, while her husband was approximately thirty years old. The man had to complete military service before he was allowed to get married. As for the girl, her parents wanted to marry her off at a very young age to protect her innocence.[5] If you think about this situation, a creep

---

5. Come on, guys, you know what I mean by that, and I'm not going to describe it any further, because if I do, all of your parents and teachers will ban this book. And if I want to go to the dollar theater and get my bucket of popcorn, I don't dare let my books get banned.

like Count Olaf had an excellent chance of marrying a fourteen-year-old Violet Baudelaire back in ancient Greece.

To make matters worse for someone like Violet, the girl was forced to marry whomever her legal male guardian decided to stick her with. So good old Count Olaf could decide to stick Violet with . . . Count Olaf.

And if that didn't seal her fate sufficiently, the ancient Greeks allowed family members to marry each other. Poor Violet would have been doomed.

In Violet's case, her father is presumed dead—burned in the fire that destroyed her home. In ancient Greece, if a girl's father croaked, all of her property as well as the right to marry her was passed to her nearest male relative. Hold on to your *Creepy!* hats, because what this means is: the ancient Greek court could have forced Klaus to marry Violet.

Let me pause here for a moment. I am a single woman; that is, I am not married. I live with my son, who is about your age, and our gigantic cat. I will die in a rocking chair with a cat on the back of my skull—hopefully, this will not happen for at least another forty or fifty years, but still—

Would I marry some strange guy for a stick of furniture? Just how badly do I crave a stool or kitchen chair?

I could use a new trash can, but still, is it worth marrying a total stranger to get a garbage receptacle?

No.

Even odder, one of the sisters had a *real* husband when she started marrying all these guys to get kitchen furniture. Here's my guess: Maybe her real husband had some kind of mental illness, whereby he had to accumulate stainless-steel garbage cans or else he'd turn into a serial killer. One could think that it would be a lot easier to earn minimum-wage pay as a garbage man—and then go out and buy stainless-steel garbage cans for yourself—than to force your wife into marrying a bunch of other men. Luckily, I do not understand the couple's logic, for if I did, it might mean that I am on my way to the loony bin, as well. At any rate, according to the newspaper, the wife divorced her real husband after her thirteenth sham wedding. Both sisters went to jail.

In London, several years ago a drug addict married twenty men to receive one million pounds, which is $1,692,421.90. The Sri Lankan mastermind of the bogus marriage racket, lawyer Mahesh Moonasinghe, earned 25,000 pounds per week by arranging sham marriages.

Of course, in soap operas—which I never watch—people routinely get married dozens of times. It would be nothing on a soap opera for an evil, old Count to marry his granddaughter, for example, while still married to his daughter and tending to her mother, whom he jailed for insanity fourteen years ago. It would be nothing for the evil, old Count to have sixteen sons by the original mother, eight daughters and six sets of twins by his next-door neighbor, and throughout it all, somehow be the wealthiest man in a huge city such as New York, London, or Los Angeles.

The actress Elizabeth Taylor has been married eight times in real life. She married and divorced actor Richard Burton twice. They starred in a movie together called *Divorce His— Divorce Hers.*

Far less well known than Taylor, who is famous for her marriages, Glynn Scotty Wolfe was married twenty-nine times. When he died at age eighty-eight in 1997, he had held the title of the world's most-married man in the Guinness Book of Records for thirty-five years. He had a son with twenty-two stepmothers. His last wife, Linda Essex-Wolfe, had been married twenty-two times before she wed Glynn Scotty. When he died, nobody stepped forward. Well, at least they didn't stuff poor Glynn Scotty into one of those sham-wedding garbage cans. There remains some dignity in this world, I suppose, even for a man who's been married twenty-nine times.

CHAPTER NINE

Picking Locks, Horseradish, and Peppermints

What do these subjects have in common? Each is part of the Lemony Snicket universe. Hence, I have grouped them all into this one, magnificent chapter:

• In Book the Third, *The Wide Window*, Violet picks the lock on Stephano's suitcase. How do real criminals pick locks? What tools do they use?

- A mini-look at horseradish—what is it, and who invented it? Why does Lousy Lane reek of fish and horseradish?
- A mini-look at allergies—what exactly *is* an allergy? Is it possible to be allergic to peppermint? If so, would you break out in rashes and double over in cramps?

I know you must be very excited, so let's get started right away with our first subject:

First Up: How to Pick a Lock

When my son, Dan, and I lived in an apartment two blocks from where we live now, there was a kid who was always trying to pick the lock of our front door. This kid would stand outside in the middle of the night—in a snowstorm wearing only a short-sleeved T-shirt, but that's another matter entirely—jamming an ordinary paper clip into our door lock. Yes, a paper clip.

Needless to say, he never broke into our apartment.

Needless to say, professional criminals do not use paper clips when trying to break into apartments.

Now if I were going to pick the lock of a suitcase, I'd probably take a huge steel hammer and break the lock. But there are other ways to pick locks.

It's actually quite easy to pick a lock. This isn't to say that you should go around picking the locks to your school, to your parent's office building, the grocery store, the gas station, the police station, the bank, and to all of your friends' houses. In fact, and trust me on this, you don't want to pick the locks of any of these places.

Also note that it is illegal to possess lock picks in some states, and also Washington, D.C. In other places, it is legal to possess picks but not to use them. If I really knew how to pick locks, I might carry a set for emergencies. But, basically, I think it's best to avoid carrying stuff like professional burglars' lock-picking sets, weapons, and other nasty things that can get you in trouble.[1]

A few weeks ago, when my son, Dan, was asleep in his bedroom with his fan rattling loudly, I couldn't get into the house. Dan had bolted the chain lock on the inside of the front door. After ten minutes of trying to awaken him by banging on the door and yelling his name, I threw my body against the door and broke the chain lock. I fell into the front hallway. So, my friends, if you don't have lock picking equipment and you're feeling desperate, you can always break a lock using my body-throwing method.[2]

Of course, thieves do not use my body-throwing method to break into buildings. They are more likely to buy lock

---

1. I'm going to give you some basic information from a guy known as Ted the Tool. It is extremely interesting that Mr. Tool warns anyone with a lock pick to "carry around a copy of the appropriate page from your state's criminal code."

2. Other methods in this category include: my break-a-window method, U.S. patent 48903Abiz2; my ax-the-door method, most definitely not recommended unless you happen to be a lumberjack; and my Advanced Go-Down-Chimney Method©®™.

picking sets for ten or twenty bucks. And they don't have to be bonded, certified, professional locksmiths.

Some picks have hooks on the end, some have balls, others have diamonds, and some have rakes. A basic set opens nearly all pin tumbler locks. I'll tell you what a pin tumbler lock is in a minute.

More lavish sets, which might cost twenty-five dollars, include picks that enable you to open most pin tumbler locks, deadbolts, doorknob locks, auto locks, and padlocks.

If someone needs to pick car locks, he can purchase a set of keys that open nearly all types of cars. He can even buy a special pick that opens the gas locks of most cars. As for cars, policemen and thieves can use a special pick that wrenches open the doors.

Now let's consider how professional locksmiths[3] use these picks. To do so, first we have to understand basic information about locks and keys.[4]

When a locksmith sticks a key into a common pin tumbler lock, he is sticking it into what is called the keyway of the plug. The keyway is the long, slender opening, and it has

---

3. . . . and police and bad guys . . .

4. Details are in Theodore T. Tool (also known as Ted the Tool), *Guide to Lock Picking*, 1991, online at www.lysator.liu.se/mit-guide. Also see: "How To Do It For Locksmiths," *Locksmith Ledger*, Des Plaines, IL, 1971; "Know How for Locksmiths", *Locksmith Ledger*, 1970; "The Lock Pick Design Manual," Paladin Press, Boulder, CO, 1975; Eddie the Wire, "How to Make Your Own Professional Lock Tools, Volume 2," Loompanics Unlimited, Port Townsend, WA, 1981.

protrusions of varying shapes and sizes. These protrusions, which we'll call pins, must be matched precisely by the key. The plug is a cylinder that rotates after the locksmith puts the correct key into the lock. Inside the keyway, the pins are numbered beginning with pin one in the front where he first inserts the key. The pin numbers increase as the key moves farther into the lock.

As the key moves into the lock, it lifts the pins. With the correct key, all pins are lifted, the plug rotates, and the lock opens. If even one pin is not lifted by the key, the plug does not rotate, and, hence, the lock does not open.

A flatland lock uses two metal plates that slide over each other only when the correct key is inserted. Without the key, the metal plates sit on top of each other in perfect alignment. The point is to slide the plates so they no longer sit exactly on top of each other. One plate should slide farther to the left, for example, than the other.

Holes are drilled into both metal plates. Pins are placed in each hole, securing the plates to each other. On the top metal plate is a spring that pushes down on the pins, and on the bottom metal plate is a protrusion that keeps the pins from falling out of the plates. The locksmith must move the pins to slide the plates over each other. To move the pins, he must insert a correct key that lifts the pins and enables the plates to move.

To pick a flatland lock without a key, the locksmith lifts each pin, one at a time. He pushes on the bottom plate, forcing one or more pins to stick between the two plates. This sticking is also known as binding the pins. If a pin is binding, the locksmith can push it up with a pick tool. Then the plates shift a bit, causing another pin to bind. So he pushes up the next pin with a pick tool, and the plates shift a bit more. And so forth, until all the pins have been lifted and the metal plates have completely shifted over each other, opening the lock.

The above technique works to open most common locks, but it takes time. There is a faster method called scrubbing. Basically, this method means that the thief—or policeman or professional locksmith—runs his pick over all of the pins. As he scrubs the pins in this fashion, the pins rise until all are up and the lock opens.

According to Ted the Tool,[5] the thief or professional lock-smith (or policeman, etc.) must insert the pick as well as a torque wrench into the lock. Without touching the pins, he must pull the pick back out of the lock while applying light pressure to the pins with the torque wrench. He then scrubs the pick over the pins while increasing the pressure he's applying to the pins with the torque wrench. The pins will start moving up and out of the way. With only a few pins left to move, he then increases the pressure with the wrench and scrubs the pins with more force. This moves the remaining pins and opens the lock.

---

5. See footnote 4 on the bottom of page 114.

There are many other tricks to picking locks, but the above information gives you the general idea.

To go with a method that does not require him to carry state and federal burglary and lock pick laws with him, the professional locksmith might procure some of the following equipment:

- Allen wrench
- File
- Screwdriver
- Paper clip (Oops, that's what the kid was using on our apartment door night after night! Maybe that kid knew what he was doing, after all!)
- Straight pin
- Safety pin
- Staple

Can you guess the role of the Allen wrench? Yes, this can be used as a torque wrench. Unfortunately, the lock-smith must grind the Allen wrench until its width is just the size to enter the keyway. If he does not own a grinder machine, then he must use something else as his torque wrench—possibly a file. Or he can use a small screwdriver or paper clip.

Now here's where the kid went wrong. In addition to the torque wrench, you need a lock pick, right? The kid only had a paper clip—no lock pick.

The locksmith can use a straight pin, safety pin, or staple

as his lock pick. With the pins, he makes sure to file off the points so he doesn't hurt himself.

If a thief does not want to be picked up by the cops and thrown in the slammer for life, and he does not have the skill to pick locks with a staple, then he sometimes makes his own picks.[6] To do this, he needs a grinder machine, as well as a pile of hacksaw blades.

After thinking about lock picks and hacksaw blades and cops and the slammer, I still vote for my tried and true techniques: body-throwing, break-the-window, and Advanced Down-the-Chimney methods. And I bet the hammer would work on the suitcase lock.

Second Up: What's Up with the Horseradish?

It comes in slender jars. Usually, it's bright red, though sometimes, it's white. Its consistency is grainy, as if someone has shaved pencils and stuck the shavings in a jar. The taste is bitter. You can't eat much of this stuff at one time.

So what is horseradish, really, and who invented it? And why does Lousy Lane reek of horseradish and fish?

Horseradish is in the mustard family. Other members of the mustard family are cauliflower, Brussels sprouts, radishes, and kale. Horseradish has thick white roots, which are

---

6. Details can be found at www.gregmiller.net/locks/.

ground into what we commonly think of as "horseradish"—the stuff in the bottles.

When you crush horseradish root cells, they release iso-thiocyanate oils, which give horseradish its characteristic odor and flavor. Manufacturers add vinegar to ground horseradish root to weaken its bite.

Along with vinegar, manufacturers may add spices, salt, sugar, and vegetable oils to horseradish. They may also add beets to it, which supply the red color seen in some variations.

Here are some interesting horseradish facts:

- Back in 1500 B.C., horseradish was used as a bitter herb by Jewish people in Egypt during Passover. It is still used as a Passover bitter herb today and symbolizes the bitter-ness of slavery and misery. Given the constant slavery and misery of the Baudelaire orphans, it makes sense that Lousy Lane reeks of horseradish. I think the other reason Lousy Lane reeks of horseradish is simply because horse-radish tastes so good with fish. However, for Lousy Lane to *reek* of horseradish implies that tons of horseradish are being manufactured and/or consumed in town.

- The ancient Greeks used horseradish as an aphrodisiac (meaning "luring someone of the opposite sex into wanting you") and as a back rubbing ointment. So if some guy wanted to date a girl back in ancient Greece, I guess he gave her a fistful of horseradish instead of flowers and candy. And if he made lewd advances and she whacked him and he fell down, twisting his back and ramming his spine against a large stone, he went home and his mother rubbed horseradish on his back.

- Between A.D. 1300 and 1600, horseradish was used in Europe to treat food poisoning, tuberculosis, colic, and scurvy.
- In the 1600s, people in England and Germany drank horseradish ale, which included wormwood and tansy. Now you might think that wormwood is a gross piece of tree bark filled with slimy worms, but it's not. Rather, it is a highly potent liquor that has a bitter anise or licorice flavor. Tansy is another wormwood plant with yellow flowers and a pleasant aroma. If you've ever eaten horseradish, you're probably wondering (as I am) how anyone could drink ale that tastes like horseradish and licorice.

Last Up: Help! I'm Allergic to Peppermint!

Everyone has allergies to something. For example, I am allergic to penicillin—and everything else that doctors have ever devised to replace penicillin. I am also allergic to bees, and if they sting me, I blow up into a giant, purplish, marbled-skin monstrosity. I've been told by doctors that the bee allergy could be fatal. Imagine that! So if a reader hates my book, he can get even by unleashing a cage of bees on me as I walk innocently down the street.[7]

Just what is an allergy? And as in the Lemony Snicket

---

7. Please don't do this to me. I promise to write better books! I swear I will!

universe, can you actually be allergic to peppermint? If so, would you break out in rashes and double over in cramps? This chapter tells all.

An allergy is an increased sensitivity or extreme reaction to a certain substance or "allergen." Some common allergens are weed pollen, ragweed, dust, pet fur and dander, wool, cosmetics, perfumes, pollen, mold, grass, trees, pollution, and feathers. I don't know about you, but I am allergic to all of these allergens, though I can manage to be around grass and trees, as long as the grass isn't dry and the trees aren't pine. I cannot wear most wool sweaters, for they make me itch. Mold drives my skin into rashes that look like abstract art paintings. Only my mother knows that I am allergic to so many things. For example, most people cannot tell that I break out in rashes when I rub against pine needles or use a soap other than Ivory. If I sneeze outside, who would know it's because the weeds and mold are particularly potent? So while we may be allergic to a lot of substances, our reactions to these substances may be fairly insignificant.

Let's suppose you are allergic to mold. You go downstairs into the basement, where the floor is coated in black slimy mold. Perhaps a previous tenant left tons of rotting, molding boxes in the basement for years, and now black slime is glued to the floor and walls.[8] As soon as your toe touches the base-

---

8. This has actually happened to me, so it's not as strange as you are thinking. Be careful. It could happen to you, too.

ment floor, you start itching and sneezing. What has happened is that your immune system has been exposed to the mold allergens, and, instantly, has started to produce antibodies. These antibodies attach themselves to cells in your skin, blood, and respiratory tract. Then the cells release chemicals, such as histamine. You start scratching your skin and sneezing.

You might note here that when you sneeze a lot, your mother may give you medicine called an antihistamine. The word *anti* means "opposite of" or "against," so in this case, the medicine "is against" the histamine that's driving you crazy.

Also, as you might have guessed, if people can be allergic to weed pollen, ragweed, dust, pet fur and dander, wool, cosmetics, perfumes, pollen, mold, grass, trees, pollution, and feathers, they can also be allergic to foods. Common food allergies include milk, eggs, wheat, nuts, chocolate, fish, and chicken.

Peppermint is a food. How likely is it that someone can be allergic to peppermint?

Peppermint, or *Nentha piperita*, is a perennial plant that has light purple flowers and green leaves. It grows to about three feet high and is found throughout North America, Europe, and Asia. More than twenty-five species of mint exist in the world.

Peppermint oil has a cool flavor and smells wonderful. Peppermint is found in toothpastes, cough drops, candies, candles, and all sorts of other things.

To reduce bloating in their stomachs, some people swallow

capsules of peppermint. Peppermint's active ingredient is menthol, which relaxes the valve between your stomach and esophagus, thus allowing gas to push upward in loud burps.

Menthol also acts as a mild anesthetic, and in lozenges, it can soothe your sore throat by numbing your throat muscles a bit.

Unless you're allergic to peppermint, the stuff is pretty safe. However, even in small amounts, undiluted peppermint oil can irritate your skin. And even in small doses, it can be toxic—that means it can kill you.

You should never ingest peppermint oil unless it is inside capsules. If you are under five years old, you shouldn't even drink peppermint tea, because it could make you choke.

A mild allergic reaction to peppermint causes skin rashes, also known as dermatitis. If you are allergic to peppermint, you could end up with red, swollen, blistered skin that itches like crazy. The blisters may even ooze fluids.

If you have a severe reaction to peppermint, you should see a doctor. He'll probably tell you to take antihistamines. He may tell you to soak in a bath.

So there you have it. You now know how to pick locks, why Lousy Lane reeks of horseradish, and whether children can really be allergic to peppermint.

CHAPTER TEN

How to Be a Lumberjack: Or the Debunking of Debarkers

The Baudelaire orphans live and work in a lumbermill throughout one entire Lemony Snicket book, *The Miserable Mill* (Book the Fourth). I've read this book at least six times, and I never get tired of it. It's incredibly funny, but also extremely sad: I can't help feeling sorry for the Baudelaires. But, then, I feel the same way when I read any Lemony Snicket book: I laugh constantly, but feel horrible for the orphans. That Snicket is a sly guy. It's rare for a book to make you laugh and feel horrible all at the same time.

Anyway, in *The Miserable Mill*, Violet, Klaus, and Sunny arrive at Paltryville, a dreary town (of course, it's dreary, as this is a Lemony Snicket book) containing the dreadful Lucky Smells Lumbermill. A guy named Phil tells them that, at the lumbermill, the children will strip bark off trees and then saw the resulting logs into boards.

Since this is one of my favorite books of all time, I naturally wanted to find out as much as possible about real lumbermills. Are debarkers real machines, or did Lemony Snicket make them up? When was the first lumbermill built? Are lumbermills as dangerous as the one Lemony Snicket describes?

First, a little background. When North America was first settled by Europeans in the 1600s through 1800s, nearly half of the continent was covered by trees. It's hard to imagine now, with our giant cities, endless suburbs, stretches of highway, and shopping malls. But long ago, forests ranged from the Atlantic Ocean clear across the country to the Mississippi River: that's 1,000 miles of forest. And in addition, southern forests stretched from Texas up to Maine for another 1,000 miles.

These trees were ancient and tall. The Pacific coast and inland mountains were covered with towering Redwoods and pines. Redwoods averaged 250 feet tall. Some were fifteen feet wide.[1]

---

1. The official name of the redwood is *Sequoia sempervirens,* named after the American Indian, Sequoya, who invented the Indian alphabet. The redwood was the tallest tree in the world, and one tree alone provided an enormous amount of lumber. The absolute tallest tree in the world is a 366-foot-high redwood called the Howard Libbey tree, and it stands in Humboldt State Park. For more about this tree, see Thomas Pakenham, *Meetings with Remarkable Trees* (New York: Random House, 1997).

A guy named A. T. Dowd discovered the Pacific coast red-woods during the Gold Rush, approximately 1850 to 1860. He was chasing a grizzly bear through the forest when he stumbled across a grove of these giant trees. When he told his buddies back at camp, they didn't believe him. They claimed he'd been drinking or perhaps he was simply out of his mind. But Dowd showed them the trees, which were each 300 feet tall with some spanning 70 feet in width. A smart man, Dowd transported cuttings, two small trees, and pockets of seed to England, where he sold his gold-mine lumber trees to the Veitch company.

The early settlers discovered that their North American trees were in high demand, not only in this country but also around the world. Hence, men began chopping down the trees, and they either sold the logs or sawed them into boards, which were termed lumber. Appropriately, these men were called lumberjacks. The trees that they cut down were called timber.

Historically, lumbermills have been located on rivers where dams provide waterpower. Approximately 1625–1635, lumbermills, then known as sawmills, first opened for business in the Northeast United States. These early sawmills produced five times more lumber than when lumberjacks just sawed the wood by hand. Basically, the mills used saws that ran up and down over the boards, all powered by water force. The logs moved on a slide beneath the saws.

Within a couple of decades, at least fifty sawmills were operating in Maine, New Hampshire, and Massachusetts. Each mill produced 500 to 1,000 feet of board every day. Soon, people lived in houses made from lumber rather than logs.[2]

Between 1800 and 1830, the United States population doubled. More timber was needed for the burgeoning population and its need for housing, barrels, carriages, poles, buildings, and other items.

When steam replaced waterpower in the 1820s, the mills picked up pace and produced five to ten times more lumber. Steam-based lumbermills meant that logging operations could move from rivers into forests and towns. By the mid-1850s, gang saws were common in the mills. With as many as twenty-four blades, a gang saw could cut an entire log into boards as quickly as one saw cut one board. With gang saws, not only did production increase, but the lumber became uniform in size: the 2' × 4' board, still common today, was one result of the gang saw.

In the mid-1850s, fifty thousand lumberjacks worked in this country, and by 1900, more than half a million people worked as loggers. New types of saws were introduced into lumbermills, enabling people to cut down trees much more quickly. In addition to the gang saw, mills used band saws at the turn of the century. These were blades on a belt running around two wheels. For more information about types of lum-

---

2. Mary Morton Cowan, *Timberrr: A History of Logging in New England* (Brookfield, CT: The Millbrook Press, 2003), p. 71.

bermill saws and boards, see "Old Lumberjack Terms" (pages 129–30). Sadly, by 1920, half of America's trees were gone.

How do you get the bark off a tree? In the Lucky Smells Lumbermill, Foreman Flacutono gives each person a large rectangle of metal that has one sharp edge. The workers grind this one sharp edge against the tree trunks to remove the bark. Because Sunny is only a baby and doesn't have the strength to lift the rectangle of metal, she uses her four baby teeth as debarkers.

Is this how real debarking is done? What *is* a real debarker? I have a theory about debarking. Because band saws are really fast, running at 3,000 feet per minute, perhaps they are used to debark a tree. You cut the tree down one side, then the other. After each cut down the length of the log, a machine rotates the log. This machine, or so I've read, has sharp teeth and shoots up from the floor.[3] Just four rotations and four long cuts, and the log loses its bark and is called a cant. Gang and band saws then cut the cant into boards.

Actually, there are machines devoted to debarking, so my theory may be one way to peel bark off a tree, but it's not the only way. For example, a Canadian lumbermill was destroyed by a fire and had to buy all new equipment. Its new setup includes a large log line and a small one. The tree-sized logs arrive at the lumbermill and are cut anywhere from 6 to 25 feet long. Logs that range up to 16 inches in diameter and up to 16 feet long enter the mill on the small log line. Then,

---

3. Ibid. (meaning the same book as in the footnote above), p. 75.

Old Lumberjack Terms

Band Saw. A saw with blades run on an endless belt over two giant wheels.

Birl. We've all seen movies or pictures of lumberjacks hopping on logs that are floating down the river. When you tread on floating logs, you're birling.

Boom. This is a good lumberjack term. It means that you chain logs together at their ends, turning them into a corral for other logs. This way, the logs don't float down the river; they're held in the boom until the sawmill's ready to ship them elsewhere.

Cant. Before being cut into boards, a log is shaved of its bark and squared off. It is then called a cant.

Cedar Savage. A debarker person: yes, a cedar savage is a person who is a real debarker. This guy peels and cuts cedar into logs and poles.

Chipper. This machine chops up bark and logs.

Circular Saw. A round steel disk with a blade around the perimeter.

Cord. A 4-foot-tall, 4-foot-wide, 8-foot-long stack of wood containing 90 cubic feet of wood and bark. Clearly, the cord hasn't come from a cedar savage, who would have peeled the bark from the tree.

Crib. Built from heavy logs and filled with stones, the crib sits on the bottom of the river. From each of its four corners, a pole rises to the surface. Lumberjacks tie booms to the poles, and they also use the cribs to sort logs. Handsome and successful loggers often appear on television shows such as *Cribs of Famous Hip-Hopping Birl-Crazy Lumberjacks.*

Crosscut Saw. Lumberjacks use these saws to cut down trees. Two men operate the crosscut saw, pulling the blade across the trunk. Before crosscut saws, lumberjacks had only their axes.

Gang Saw. A series of parallel saws in one big cutting mechanism.

Jack Ladder. Long chain used to haul logs out of the water to the saws.

Kerf. The width of the cut made by a saw blade. A kerf-few is a small cut.

Log Jammer. When logs are jammed while floating down the river, this guy breaks up the mess.

Long Johns. Long, heavy underwear. I put this term into the list just to see if you're awake.

Mill Scale. The board feet of logs sent to the lumbermill.

River Drive. Floating logs down the river to the lumbermill.

according to www.forestnet.com,[4] two 18-inch Cambio debark-ers remove the bark from the logs. At this point, the logs are processed by a variety of machines: a Swecan canter, a Co-mact circular twin, a vertical arbor edger. For big cants (see "Old Lumberjack Terms" on page 129), the automatic ma-chinery sends logs to a Ukiah 12-inch-by-54-inch double ar-bor edger. Now I don't know what any of these machines do, of course, and while I could find out and let you know, it's enough for me to know that debarker machines exist. Do we really need details about the Kockums chipper edger? And it gets even more involved when we talk about how the larger logs are processed. They go through a 30-inch Cambio de-barker, a Forano headrig, with cants going to a Ukiah double arbor edger and sideboards to a Kockums chipping edger. If that weren't enough equipment, all the lumber is then trimmed with multi-saw trimming machines and then sorted and processed.

The debarker itself may be one of many models from one of many different manufacturers. Many debarkers remove the bark from hardwoods, softwoods, cedars, and cypress trees. They handle log diameters from 6 inches on up, and they op-erate by electric motors.

Now, do pinchers really exist, as they do in the Lemony

---

4. Tony Kryzanowski, "Coming Back Strong," *Logging and Sawmilling Journal,* at www.forestnet.com.

Snicket lumbermill? Mr. Snicket knows his lumbermill lore. As with debarkers, there are also pinchers in the mills. They are stuck on the ends of large hydraulic and electric arms. They look like metal claws, and they enable the lumbermill operator to pick up logs, scrap, and wood debris. This is exactly what happens in the Lucky Smells Lumbermill. The pinchers grab and lift trees from piles, then dump them in the debarking location.

And as in the Lucky Smells Lumbermill, real lumbermills are very dangerous places. Men can lose their arms and legs. Men can lose their heads. Literally.

Sometimes, people fall into the circular and band saws. Other times, boards konk their heads, saws throw wood at their necks and chests, and log chains go haywire, wrap around guys, and kill them. And of course, like all equipment, saws break. When this happens, the mill becomes extremely dangerous. If a piece of metal, such as a sugar maple nail, grinds into a saw blade, the saw might hurl wood around the mill, killing guys. If a saw catches a scrap of cloth on a guy's pants leg, he probably loses his leg, and maybe he loses more than his leg.

The most famous lumberjack of all time was Paul Bunyan. He was taller than redwood trees, and he could cut down an entire forest using his three-mile-long saw. He traipsed around the country with his giant ox, Babe. And he carved out the Grand Canyon using only his ax. Of course, Paul Bunyan wasn't quite . . . real.

Another famous lumberjack, though not nearly as well known as Paul Bunyan, was Jimmy Stewart; not the Jimmy Stewart of old-times movie fame, but, rather, a real guy who was a real lumberjack. This particular Jimmy Stewart was a champion birler, which means he could remain standing on floating logs longer than anyone else. Tall tales rose about this famous birler, and the tall tales, of course, were not true. For example, lumberjacks liked to tell the story of when Jimmy Stewart birled for two straight days to win a contest against a guy named Tom Oliver, who fell asleep after two days of hip-hopping on his log.

Jigger Jones, who wielded his ax in the late 1800s, worked in the freezing forests of Maine. Yet he never wore shoes or a coat. He only wore Long Johns (if you don't know what Long Johns are, see "Old Lumberjack Terms" on page 130) and a pair of pants. Jigger started working at a logging camp when he was twelve years old. He was tiny and had scars all over his body. The scars were from the spikes on the bottoms of other guys' shoes. The other loggers would throw Jigger into the snow and jump on him, digging spikes into his body. Jigger even fell from a 45-foot-tall dam, yet he always managed to survive. In fact, Jigger Jones was a lumberjack for forty years.

Today's lumberjack is a lot different from Paul Bunyan, Jimmy Stewart, or Jigger Jones. He rarely uses an ax, he doesn't drive logs down the river, and he probably doesn't live in logging camps with a hundred other lumberjacks.

Today's lumberjack uses chain saws to chop down trees.

He transports logs using tractors. He hauls logs out of the woods through the sky, using thick cables. He uses cranes to lift dozens of logs at once.

At the modern lumbermill are automatic conveyer belts, saws, and sanders for smoothing the wood. Computers run all the equipment. There are a few people around the mill, but, mostly, they aren't in pits, holding dangerous saws and hoping metal bolts don't fly into the saws, causing wood to catapult across the mill and decapitate their buddies. It's not as dangerous as it used to be, though, as mentioned above, the dangers are all still there.

As I close this chapter, I must talk about some of the world's largest and most ancient trees. Most books, stories, and magazine articles that discuss logging and lumbermills end on a somber note. They bemoan the loss of the forest and apologize for the destruction of trees. Ecology and environmental issues are briefly described. I do not want to write about the sad destruction of the world's forests. I'd rather focus on more cheerful topics, such as ancient and really cool trees that have *not* been chopped down by loggers.

For example, in the White Mountains in California, some of the trees are more than 4,000 years old.[5] The oldest tree in the world sits there, more than 4,600 years old: imagine

---

5. Notes about giant and weird trees are drawn from the excellent *Meetings with Remarkable Trees* (New York: Random House, 1997) by Thomas Pakenham.

any living thing on this planet that is 4,600 years old. It's truly extraordinary to ponder. This ancient tree is a bristle-cone pine (*Pinus longaeva*), and with it are seventeen other bristlecone pines more than 4,000 years old.

You might guess that these trees are sky high. If so, you are wrong. They grow high in the mountains—10,000 feet up, and they are buried in snow and ice. They grow very slowly because it's only for a few weeks every year that they get enough sun and water. Basically, they survive by sucking up melting snow. So the trees are stunted in appearance: that is, they are squat, short, and gnarled. They are not at all sky high.

In Japan, the widest-trunk trees are camphors (*Cinnamomum camphora*), a type of evergreen. Shrines are built adjacent to the trees, and tourists come by the busload to worship the trees. The trees are considered sacred, and if you walk around them in a complete circle, it is said that one year is added to your life.

In Australia, the mountain ash (*Eucalyptus regnans*) used to grow from 350 to 400 feet tall. Logging didn't leave any of the giants, though in 1930, there was still one tree that was 70 feet in diameter. Today, the largest diameter of an Australian mountain ash trunk is only 30 feet.

In Madagascar, ancient baobab trees grow into the forms of sweet potatoes, bottles, demons, and other strange things. The trees grow up to 40 feet high and have a pink cast to them.

There are a lot of other cool, old trees, somehow spared the logger's ax and saw. But, mostly, trees have died to give us homes, furniture, and paper, and simply to clear the earth for communities to grow. I guess it's pretty sad to think about debarkers, pinchers, and all of those other lumbermill machines, as now they seem like tree torture machines to me.

CHAPTER ELEVEN

Do Not Read This Chapter Until I Snap My Fingers

DISCLAIMER: If you fall asleep while reading this chapter, it isn't because I hypnotized you. If your friends tell you tomorrow that you slumped in your chair, dropped this book, and then squawked like a chicken, it isn't because I hypnotized you. Now I'm going to count to three very slowly, and then I'm going to snap my fingers . . .

At the Lucky Smells Lumbermill, Klaus is hypnotized by Count Olaf and his pals. Is hypnosis real, and if so, how is it done? Can anyone be hypnotized? When you're hypnotized, do you walk around in a stupor? Finally, how do you break real hypnotic spells? This chapter answers these questions, and more.

The traditional notion of hypnosis is that a person goes into a trance, or falls asleep, and the hypnotist makes the person squawk like a chicken, forget who he is, become a thief, or do something else contrary to the person's ordinary state of being. To debunk this classic idea, some professional hypnotists claim that hynopsis is a self-help condition, whereby a person daydreams in a positive way. The professional, who, after all, doesn't want us to think he's a seller of snake oil medicines or that he's going to make us turn into thieves, goes so far as to claim that we are in a hypnotic trance when we watch an engrossing movie or read a book. I don't quite buy that idea. But let's explore it further.

The professional who ascribes to this theory, that hypnosis is like a positive daydream or some sort of guided meditation, explains that a person in an hypnotic state has slowed his brain waves from beta to alpha waves. The alpha brain waves are the ones we experience during sleep.

According to professional hypnotists,[1] the brain has four

---

1. G. Edward Riley, Certified Master Hypnotist, and C. J. Newton, Master Hypnotherapist, TherapistFinder.net Mental Health Journal, April 2001.

states corresponding to frequencies of electrical activity in the brain: Full Conscious Awareness, the Hypnotic state, the Dream state, and the Sleep state.

Full Conscious Awareness has electrical brain activity in the range of 14 to 35 hertz and is known as your beta state. The Hypnotic, or alpha state, is at 8 to 13 hertz. The Dream, or theta state, is at 4 to 7 hertz, and the Sleep, or delta state, is at 0.5 to 3 hertz.

Hertz, by the way, may be a rental car agency, but it also measures things such as your brain waves. More specifically, it measures the frequency of wave patterns in cycles per second.

When you are fully conscious, your brain waves are cruising at 14 to 35 hertz in the beta state, and when you are hypnotized, your brain waves slow down to 8 to 13 hertz. You're not quite asleep, not dreaming, not dead to the world. But you're not awake, either.

When in the Hypnotic state, the theory is that the door between your conscious everyday state and your dreamy, sleepy, subconscious state opens. People, such as hypnotists, can then ask you questions, and you can go through your subconscious doorway into your memories and get the answers. These are memories and answers not available to your conscious, everyday, awake state.

So you're not really thinking about how to answer the hypnotist's questions. You aren't analyzing what you're doing, what he's asking, what you're about to say: you're simply experiencing the whole thing and reacting to suggestions made to you.

In some form or another, hypnosis has been around for a long time. For example, in 1766, Franz Anton Mesmer obtained a degree in medicine and started using hypnotism to help cure his patients. He treated a blind woman named Maria Teresa Paradis, and, supposedly using hypnotism, gave her vision again. How entering a state between fully conscious and dreaming can restore vision is unknown to me. Yet people have claimed to be able to do this type of thing for hundreds of years. Actually, in 1784, Mesmer was pronounced a fraud.

Has anything unusual struck you about Mesmer's name? Klaus would probably tell you that Mesmer's work in mesmerizing people led to the word *mesmerized*. This is true. To mesmerize someone is to put him under a spell, to hypnotize him in a way. For many years, hypnosis was called mesmerism.

In 1841, an English physician named James Braid began studying hypnotism and experimenting with it on his patients. At the time, hypnotism was still called mesmerism. It was Dr. Braid who renamed the technique to call it hypnotism, after the Greek word *hypnos*, which means "sleep." He later realized that hypnotism wasn't really a sleep state, but, rather, a condition between the conscious and unconscious.

Other doctors studied hypnotism, but it wasn't until Sigmund Freud came along that anyone truly famous studied the technique. He studied with Dr. Hippolite Berhmeim and Dr. Jean-Martin Charcot. Dr. Charcot maintained that only weak and very nervous people could be hypnotized. Freud dabbled with hypnosis, but eventually dropped it because he wasn't able to induce hypnotic trances in his patients.

In 1955, the British Medical Association formally approved of the use of hypnosis in medicine. And in 1958, the American Medical Association also approved of hypnosis as a medical tool. Clearly, there is validity to hypnosis, and we should take it very seriously.

When someone hypnotizes you, he can make your muscles rigid or relaxed, remove your pain, or induce great pain in your body. He can make you taste salt as sugar, and sugar as vinegar. He can make you think that beautiful music is raucous shrieking, and vice versa. He can make you talk in strange ways. He can reach into your innermost being and change or remove your fears, anxieties, and other emotional problems. The hypnotist can suggest that your legs are relaxing, and your legs do relax; that your eyelids are growing heavy, and they do shut; that you're going into a deep, deep sleep, and you do fall into a slumber-like state.

Your body relaxes. Your mind is able to focus very clearly. You are very susceptible to the suggestions of the hypnotist.

One common fallacy is that you cannot leave the hypnotic trance once you are in it; that only the hypnotist can let you out of the trance. According to professional hypnotists, this is not always the case. If a hypnotist asks a person to shoot his dog, for example, the person may jerk awake and completely leave the hypnotic state. And then he will fire the hypnotist. So it's quite possible that Klaus could have come out of his hypnotic state long before his hypnosis actually broke.

The first thing to do when trying to hypnotize someone is to make the person feel very relaxed. We'll pretend for this discussion that you are going to hypnotize your friend, Harry. To start removing Harry's tension about being hypnotized, say something like, "Please stand up. We're going to do a couple of tests just to see how you respond. I am not going to try to hypnotize you."

After Harry stands, and after you tell him to stop snickering and to take things seriously, tell him to stare at something on the wall in front of him. If you're in the living room, for example, and your mother has a photo of you as a baby on the wall over the sofa, ask Harry to stare at your baby picture. If your Uncle Moe has a giant black velvet Elvis painting on the wall behind Aunt Hilda's rocking chair, ask Harry to stare at Elvis. If there's nothing on a wall anywhere in your house, then maybe you should get hypnotized and find out why you're living in a totally sterile environment.

With Harry staring at, say, your baby photo on the wall, put your hands on Harry's shoulders and say, "Lean back into my hands."

After Harry leans gently into your hands, let him fall slowly backwards about eight inches, then gently push him upright so he's standing again.

Repeat this procedure two or three times.

Now put your arms straight over Harry's shoulders. Make sure your arms do not touch Harry. Your palms should face upwards and your fingers should be slightly curled.

Using your sternest mother or father tone, chastise Harry

for giggling and not taking the hypnosis session seriously. Point out that the hypnosis won't work unless Harry cooperates and truly believes in your ability to hypnotize him. If he does not behave, threaten to start the process over. If he still does not behave, threaten to make him stare at the Elvis painting for four hours. If he still does not behave, give up and find another friend to hypnotize. It is crucial that your friend believe in your ability to put him into a hypnotic trance.

So if all is working out well, and Harry is trying to relax and take things seriously, ask him now to stare at your fingers, which are curled in front of his face. Say, "Stare at my fingers. As I bring them toward you, let the invisible power push you back toward me. As my fingers come closer, and now closer, to your eyes, fall backwards into my arms." Continue to say similar things, such as "Fall backwards, backwards into my arms. You are drifting backwards, backwards. The invisible force pushes you back and now farther back." Let your voice sound dreamy.

Things are going well, and Harry drops into your arms. Then he straightens up, feeling embarrassed and silly. Tell Harry he's doing a fine job.

Ask Harry to face you. Keeping your elbows at your sides, raise your hands with your palms facing up. Tell Harry to put his hands in yours. Tell Harry to relax. Now pull your hands from beneath Harry's hands. Do his hands drop to his sides? If so, he is relaxed enough for the next step. If not, repeat this procedure a few more times until Harry's hands simply drop to his sides when you pull your hands away.

And now you are ready to hypnotize Harry. Do not tell Harry that he will now be hypnotized. Just do it.

Ask Harry to sit in a comfortable chair. Ask him to keep his arms relaxed at his sides without his hands touching. Sit across from him in another comfortable chair. Make sure the chairs are fairly close.

Tell Harry to look directly over him at the ceiling. Ask him to choose a spot on the ceiling. Now tell him to stare at that spot.

After a short while, say a minute or two, when Harry's eyes are probably getting tired from staring at a spot on the ceiling, begin talking in your dream-state voice. Say something like this: "Stare at the spot on the ceiling. Keep your eyes focused on that spot on the ceiling. Now let your shoulders relax. Relax every muscle in your shoulders. Let the relaxation melt through your shoulders, melt, melt until the muscles in your upper arms relax, too. Let the relaxation melt through your upper arms, drip, drip farther down your arms, relaxing your elbows, your forearms, your fingers. Stare at the spot on the ceiling. Concentrate on relaxing your shoulders and arms. Your arms are growing limp. Your eyes are growing tired. Your body is growing tired. Your eyelids want to shut. Feel the relaxation melt farther down from your shoulders and arms, into your chest, now into your stomach. Your leg muscles are relaxing, going limp. Your eyes are tired. Your eyelids must close. Just let your eyelids close, let your eyes rest, they are so tired, close them, feel them closing, closing . . . now let them stay closed."

If Harry's eyes are still open, start again, directing him to relax his shoulder muscles, his arm muscles, and onwards down his body, until he relaxes his leg muscles, as well. Keep telling him to let his eyelids shut.

When finally, Harry's eyelids are closed and he is totally relaxed, you can commence the hypnotic session.

There are many other methods of inducing hypnosis in Harry, of course. The most famous method is to stand a couple of feet away from him and stare into his eyes. Ask Harry to take a deep breath and hold it, now a second deep breath, and to hold that one, too. As Harry's holding his breath a second time, lift your hands over his head. As Harry exhales, lower one of your hands in front of Harry's eyes and lower the other hand behind his head to his neck. Do not touch him. Now say something like, "I'm going to count down from five to one. When I reach the number one, you will enter a deep state of hypnosis, falling deeply into sleep, more deeply than you've ever slept before. Five. Four. Three. Two. And one."

When you reach the number one, pull Harry's head forward with the hand you have placed behind his head. Say in a deep voice, "*Sleep.*" Pull Harry's head onto your shoulder. Massage his neck muscles. Now say the same relaxation statements you used before: tell Harry to relax his shoulders, then his arms, his chest, and, finally, his legs. As he slumps, ease him gently back into a comfortable chair.

Regardless of the method you use to hypnotize Harry, you now want to make sure that he's truly in an hypnotic trance.

The trance itself may be anywhere from light to medium to deep to what is called esdaile.

If Harry's in a light hypnotic trance, his eyelids may be fluttering and he appears relaxed. It wouldn't take much to break the trance. If his breathing is extremely relaxed and slow and his arms and legs are limp, then the trance is a bit deeper. If you ask Harry to lift an arm, he won't be able to do it without enormous effort.

If Harry's in a medium hypnotic trance, then his arms are completely limp and he will be unable to lift them. His speech is slow, drowsy, trancelike. In this condition, Harry is susceptible to whatever you ask him to do, barring requests that he commit crimes or do other dangerous or bad things. Even in an hypnotic state, people do not do things they know to be wrong.

If Harry's in a deep hypnotic trance, his lips will be parted, his face will be pale. He will do anything you tell him to do, including changing his personality. For example, if Harry gets D's in school, you can get him to study really hard and get B's while he's hypnotized. If Harry eats too many french fries and is a lazy slob, you can get him to eat Brussels sprouts and jog. In this state, you can make Harry return to when he was five years old, remember things he thought he'd forgotten from when he was a toddler. You can make him squawk like a chicken. If he's been in a lot of pain, say from a broken leg or stomach food poisoning, you can make that pain go away.

In the esdaile state, Harry's got trouble. Most professional hypnotists do not attempt to put their patients into this condition. It is very dangerous and attempts to use hypnotic trances instead of anesthetics during major operations. Yes, this is true—I'm not even kidding around. Do not attempt to put your friend, Harry, into an esdaile state, please!

Actually, this state was named after Dr. James Esdaile, who performed hundreds of serious operations on people who were without anesthesia but who were in hypnotic trances.

In the early 1800s when Esdaile was practicing medicine, no anesthesia was available. Patients underwent surgery without the help of drugs, for the most part, so even hypnosis was better than nothing. It was worth the risk. After all, 40 percent of people died due to surgical procedures back then, so anything that helped was worth trying. Hence, using hypnosis as anesthesia, Esdaile amputated limbs, removed cataracts from eyes, removed tumors from his patients' bodies, and performed operations on various body organs.

Perhaps this early use of hypnotism during surgery spawned the wave of horror films and novels that portray hypnotists as evil monsters, cult leaders, and mad scientists. Here, the hypnotist has bulging eyeballs, a deep voice, and the charm of Dr. Evil. He sucks poor, innocent people under his spell, making them do terrible things, making them rob, set fires, murder. He makes people into his slaves.

In George du Maurier's novel *Trilby*, the hypnotist Svengali turned a shy woman into a magnificent opera star. The novel was made into a movie in 1931, with Svengali played by the famous actor John Barrymore. In the film, Svengali was no self-help healer. Instead, he was portrayed as a greedy, manipulative con artist.

In the classic 1957 movie, *I Was a Teenage Werewolf*, an evil hypnotist turned a kid into an apelike monster who killed his high school buddies. The kid just wanted to be more popular and get better grades. He thought hypnosis might turn him from a shy and awkward kid with average grades into a super-hunk jock-boy with genius grades. But in the hands of an evil hypnotist, he was turned into a killer werewolf.

In *Horrors of the Black Museum*, which was released in 1959, a writer hypnotized his assistant to kill people. The writer got all his plot and character ideas by recording what his assistant did. As a writer, I see two flaws with this movie. First, in the movie, the writer has an assistant, which is ridiculous. Trust me on this, I have no assistant except for my cat, who cannot be hypnotized to kill anybody. My cat is always in a deep, trancelike state anyway, and when she's not in deep sleep, she's eating chow or chasing birds. No way can she be hypnotized to kill the mailman, so I can get ideas for my dreadful books. Oh, which brings me to the second point: my books are so bad that, clearly, I do not get plot and character ideas from any source outside my own head.

Of course, there have been many other horror films and novels featuring evil hypnotists. All vampires hypnotize their victims, just to name one obvious example. The victim looks into the vampire's eyes, instantly falls under his spell, and while in an hypnotic trance is drained of blood. A few hypnosis films that come to mind are *The Hypnotic Eye*, *The Hypnosis Murder*, and *Incredibly Strange Creatures Who Stopped Living and Became Mixed-Up Zombies*.

CHAPTER TWELVE

Work, Slave, Work!
Child Labor Laws

Do child labor laws protect real children from working in lumbermills, schools, offices, and other places? What is the history behind current child labor laws? Can a fourteen-year-old, a twelve-year-old, and a baby legally work as lumbermill employees? Can Sunny, the baby, be Vice Principal Nero's secretary?

By 1900, child labor in this country was booming. Children as young as toddlers worked in factories, mills, canneries, fields, and coal mines. In fact, by 1900, more than two million kids under sixteen years old worked six days a week, twelve hours a day. They earned poverty wages. And they worked under very dangerous conditions.

The world of the Baudelaire orphans was very real back then. Children were slave laborers. Three-year-old toddlers, just out of babyhood, picked cotton in the fields. Twelve-year-old kids worked the night shifts in the factories. Boys picked slate from coal with bleeding fingers, or they descended into the mines every day to dig coal from the ground. Girls worked in the spinning rooms of cotton mills, with cold water thrown at their faces to keep them awake during their long work shifts. Toddlers worked in sweatshop factories: yes, toddlers. As soon as they could walk, kids transported clothing and other goods across town. They tended dangerous machines in work environments where they could barely breathe.

At the turn of the century, things were bad for kids in this country. People were so poor that they were forced to send their children to work. Parents earned such low wages that families would starve without the money earned by the children. And orphans were everywhere, with no place to live and nothing to eat unless they earned money on their own.

Entire immigrant families lived in dilapidated shacks in cannery labor camps. The shacks were infested with rats and roaches, they were filthy, and they had no water. Immigrants moved from one cannery labor camp to another, as the work drifted from place to place. In the North, they picked peaches and strawberries, then they drifted South to harvest shrimps and oysters. Work began at approximately 3 A.M. and didn't cease until late at night. Because parents and children worked together, even babies were present at 3 A.M. for the never-ending work shift of shucking oysters, shelling shrimps, picking peaches, picking berries. As soon as a baby could waddle around and use a knife without killing himself, he was put to work in the cannery camps. For working a twelve-hour shift, a child might receive ten cents a day.

At this time, reformers rose up against the child slavery, claiming that children have the right to be just children. Formed in 1904, the National Child Labor Committee began campaigning against child labor and tried to outlaw the practice. The Committee wanted to ban children from working in dangerous places. They also wanted to ban employment of children less than fourteen years old from most jobs. They demanded that children work no more than eight hours per day, that children not be given the night factory shifts, and that children be forced under law to attend school. They felt that only through education would children have any chance whatsoever to grow up and have a decent life. If kids worked from the age of three up rather than going to school, then as adults, they would continue to live in poverty.

The fight to limit child labor included the fight to help orphans. After all, if a four-year-old girl had no home and no parents, and she had to sell flowers to earn money for a piece of bread, who could possibly argue that she shouldn't have the right to do it? The only reasonable argument was that she should (a) have the right not to work, and (b) also have the right to shelter and food from the society around her. This was about the time, as we discussed in our chapter about orphans, that orphanages and adoption laws began to emerge. The orphanages were bleak and miserable, too, of course; and as we mentioned earlier in this book, orphans often were rounded up and shipped out West on orphan trains; but still, it beat living on the cold streets of New York City in the dead of winter. How much bread can you buy from the sale of a flower?

My grandfathers were immigrants, who started working full-time (or more) as tailors at the age of thirteen. After escaping from Russia and then learning the tailor trade in Italy, they came to America in their teens to get jobs in New York City. They never went to school. My grandmother worked in a doll factory and never learned to speak the English language. My other grandmother never knew English, either, and while she raised eight children in a one-room apartment beneath a railroad track in New York City, she never worked outside of her home. During the Great Depression, my mother's family had to live on the beach because they couldn't afford rent. Both she and my aunt went to work as kids to earn money to support the family. My father sold eggs door to door, trying to earn a buck. Times were tough following World War I and during the Great Depression.

Just based on my own family's history, it seems likely that

immigrant poverty, lack of education, and then World War I followed by the Great Depression all created a vast underclass of working children. And this was in the 1930s, long after the founding of the National Child Labor Committee in 1904.

Still, in the first decade of the 1900s, states began passing laws to limit the working hours and wages of children. But the states rarely enforced their own child labor laws, and manufacturers, factory owners, cotton-field and coal-mine owners, and other wealthy adults continued to take advantage of children.

In 1908, Georgia tried to introduce a strong child labor law, but the wealthy mill owners in the state made sure the law was never passed. They forced impoverished people to sign long petitions against the child labor laws. Most of the people signed with an X because they did not know how to sign their own names.

Despite the efforts of the National Child Labor Committee, children continued to fall prey to the harsh working environments: tuberculosis and bronchitis were common. Children working in mills were half as likely to reach the age of twenty than children who did not have to work.

Possibly the worst cases of child labor were in coal mines, where boys from nine to fourteen years of age slaved away as mule drivers, runners, spraggers, couplers, and gate tenders. Little boys worked in the coal breakers outside of the mines. They removed slate and stone from coal as it poured out of chutes into giant holding bins beneath them. Thick, black dust billowed everywhere, making it hard to see and even more difficult to breathe. Because the coal kept flowing from the chutes into the bins, quite often boys slipped into the stream of coal beneath their feet and were smothered to death or mangled.

As soon as a boy was twelve, he had to leave the breaker and work in the coal mines. Here, explosions killed people, and caves collapsed on them. It was a lonely, miserable existence.

In addition to working in fields, mines, and factories, children labored on the streets of American cities. They peddled newspapers, ribbons, candy, flowers, shoelaces. They shined shoes. They hauled firewood and ice. They worked in city sweatshops. Many of these children were homeless orphans, much like the Baudelaires. In fact, in New York City alone, there were many thousands of impoverished, working orphans living on the streets.

In 1916 and 1918, Congress passed child labor laws aimed at protecting children all over America: in rural factories, mills, and fields; and on the streets of the cities. But the U.S. Supreme Court declared that the laws were unconstitutional: it was up to the states, declared the Supreme Court, to decide the fate of their children; and it was up to the children to decide if they needed to work to get money for food.

Then in 1924, Congress tried again by suggesting a Constitutional amendment that would allow the government to create child labor laws. But again the attempt failed. After ten years of trying to pass the amendment, Congress gave up.

During the Great Depression, adults started taking jobs from children. There simply were no jobs, so competition was fierce even for the most horrible, low-paying positions. As young teenagers, my mother and aunt were lucky to get jobs during that time. My mother tells the story of how she competed for a temporary store clerk's job against thousands of men and women, all of whom were much older. And, as mentioned, my father peddled eggs door to door.

Finally, in 1938, President Roosevelt signed the Fair Labor Standards Act, which, among other things, limited child labor. For example, if under the age of sixteen, children were not allowed to work in manufacturing and mining operations. They could still work on farms, however.

In 1949, Congress amended the Fair Labor Standards Act to mandate that children under sixteen could not work in commercial agriculture, transportation, public utilities, and communications companies.

Today, federal law prohibits children from working during school hours. Also, the law prohibits children from working full-time after school and on weekends.

While I'm sure sweatshop labor still exists, particularly for immigrants and the desperate impoverished, the plight of the Baudelaire orphans seems unreasonable. Legally, they would not be allowed to work in a preparatory school, in a lumber-mill, or any other sweatshop environment. Legally, they would have to go to school, just like you. In this way, the law would protect them.

CHAPTER THIRTEEN

Crabs, Fungi, Staples, and Leeches

What do these subjects have in common? Each is part of the Lemony Snicket universe. Hence, in this chapter, we talk about crabs and where they live: could they actually live away from the ocean in a tin shack at Prufrock Prep? We also talk about fungus and take a stab at identifying the type of fungus that's growing on the ceiling of the shack. We look at staples: is it possible for Sunny to make staples manually—that is, without using any tools? This chapter gives you some background about how staples were first used, who invented them, and how staplers came to exist. And, finally, this chapter tells you the gross truth about leeches.

First Up: Prufrock Prep Crabs

In this section, we delve into the crabs that live in the tin shack at Prufrock Preparatory School. Most of us think that crabs live in the ocean or on the beaches, where there's lots of water. So how can crabs live in a shack at the Prufrock School? And if it is possible for crabs to live on land, can they be the size of match boxes, as in the Lemony Snicket books? What do these weird crabs eat, how did they get there, how do they survive?

First, we'll talk about crabs, in general: what they are, where they live, what they do for fun on the weekends.

Scientists lump crabs into a group called decapod crustaceans. A crustacean wears a hard shell and has a segmented body. The segments are called somites, and they are fused together along the crustacean's body. Its limbs usually have two main segments. If you, as a human, were a crustacean, your forearm and upper arm would count as the two main segments. However, unlike crabs and other crustaceans, you do not have antennae on your head; crustaceans have two pairs of antennae. And unlike you, the human, the crustacean has gills for breathing—just like fish.

At this point, you're probably thinking, if the crab has gills, then how could it possibly live on land in the tin shack at Prufrock Preparatory School? Wouldn't all crabs have to live in the ocean, or at least in my backyard swimming pool?

Surprise! Yes, although crustaceans originally lived only in the ocean, explaining the gills, many have adapted to life on land.

Decapods have five pairs of walking limbs, or ten limbs total. They include not only crabs, but also lobsters, shrimps, and crayfish. In the case of the crab, the first pair of limbs—the ones closest to the eye stalks and four antennae—are huge and have giant pinchers on the ends. Some have paddles on the ends of their hind legs to help them swim.

Some interesting facts about crabs are:

- They shed their external shells
- They have compound eyes on movable eyestalks
- They can regenerate lost limbs.

Shrimps have legs beneath their abdomens which help them swim. Some shrimp, and all crayfish, only swim backwards using their long tails. This way, they can swim very quickly away from predators while battling the predators with their claws.

In addition, the tail sweeps water into their gills and food into their mouths. If you want to learn about shrimp, see the box "Ghost and Zombie Shrimp" (page 161).

For all crustaceans—shrimps, crayfish, lobsters, and crabs—the front antenna not only help them find their way, but they also serve as the animals' sensory organs. It's really weird but true: inside the antenna are the crab's taste cells, called aesthetasks.

The eyes and eyestalks are pretty cool, too. Each eyestalk contains big, bulging compound eyes that each have from 7,000 to 30,000 eye facets, called onmatids.

The shell itself is made from chitin and also contains calcium carbonate for added strength. The crab's muscles are attached to its shell, and on the inside the shell is held together by a layer of skin.

Because the crab grows quickly, it sheds its shell often. In fact, it is constantly growing a soft, new shell beneath its current one. When the crab is ready to *molt* (another word for "shed") its current shell, its eyestalks release hormones that deplete their appetite. So the crab stops eating and goes on a starvation diet. Being skinny, the crab easily squirms from its old shell. Sometimes, though, limbs get stuck in the old shell and rip from the crab's body.

After molting the old shell, the crab is covered by its soft, new shell. This means prey can attack it more easily. It no longer has the hard shell protecting its body.

In addition, after shedding the old shell, the crab is exhausted. Imagine if you had to starve practically to death to become really skinny, then shed your entire body skin, leaving you coated only by an extremely thin skinlike mesh. You'd be exhausted and sickly, too.

Ghost and Zombie Shrimp

Ghost shrimp are tiny and nearly transparent. For example, the Florida Ghost Shrimp is only 6 centimeters long, while the even smaller Glass Shrimp and Paraguay Ghost Shrimp measure only 4 centimeters. But even these shrimp are big brutes compared to the 3-centimeter-long Palenque Floating Shrimp in Mexico.

Larger fish prey on them, and they exist mainly as scavengers. Being nearly transparent, tiny scavengers—not exactly strong, handsome, aggressive fish—it's no wonder the ghost shrimp are so ghostlike, hiding under plants and rocks, hoping nobody sees them.

Forgive me, but I made up the bit about the Zombie Shrimp. I do not know of shrimps who resemble zombies, unless of course we are referring to the ghost shrimps, who pretend to be dead all the time so they won't be eaten by everything else in the water.

So the crab just lies around, half dead, after shedding its old shell. It may eat its old shell. It may just hide and eat nothing, waiting for its new shell to harden. Not only do prey come after the crab during this time, but even other crabs may try to attack and kill it.

If the crab's old limbs got caught in the old shell and

ripped off, then the crab grows new limbs. Within days or weeks, the crab's new shell hardens, and by then, its new limbs are also in place.

Land crabs may have gills, but they do spend most of their time outside of the water. They eat vegetables, for the most part, but will also eat small fish and meats.

Land crabs come in all different colors, and most are quite small: matchbox-sized, perhaps. The Rainbow Land Crab from Brazil, to name one example, can be orange and purple, or it can be pink, green, blue, yellow, and orange. It truly looks like a rainbow. However, it is 20 centimeters long, which is approximately 7.8 inches, a wee bit larger than a matchbox.

The Costa Rican Land Crab is gray and brown, and it's 30 centimeters long, considerably bigger than a matchbox. It's unlikely that the Baudelaires encountered either the Brazilian or Costa Rican Land Crabs in their tin shack.

The beautiful blue, purple, and green Belem Long Arm Land Crab from Brazil would make for a playful pet in the tin shack. But, alas, it is also too long: 25 centimeters.

Indonesian crabs are also too long at 20 centimeters, as are the Malawi Blue Land Crabs. It doesn't seem as if land crabs are the size of matchboxes, does it?

If there's salty water around the tin shack, then there's a chance that matchbox-sized crabs live at Prufrock Prep. As luck would have it, the Red Fiddler Crab from South Asia is . . . get ready for this! . . . only 5 centimeters long. That means the Red Fiddler Crab is 1.9 inches long, the size of a matchbox.

The little Red Fiddler is a pretty shade of reddish orange and has huge yellow pinchers. It prefers warm weather, thriving in temperatures between 71 and 77 degrees Fahrenheit. These crabs would probably die in the winter in North America.

It is my guess that Klaus, Violet, and Sunny are living with South Asian Red Fiddler Crabs. They may also be the 4-centimeter-long Red Claw Crabs from South Asia, but I rather like the thought of living with Fiddler Crabs instead, who sound more musical and fun than the evil-sounding Claw Crabs.[1]

Both the Red Fiddler and Red Claw Crabs like to crawl out of the water and hang out on sand, rocks, gravel, and dirt. But they do enjoy the water, too, so my guess is that there's a brackish pool of water nearby. (*Brackish* means that the water is salty, but not quite as salty as marine or ocean water.)

By the way, if both Red Fiddler and Red Claw Crabs live in the shack together, then the orphans are going to be watching some brutal crab fights. And, basically, the evil-sounding Claws are going to be slaughtered by the musical-sounding Fiddlers.

Let's assume the Fiddlers are everywhere in the shack, scampering sideways all over the walls and ceiling. They do happen to move sideways, by the way. Their limbs bend as

---

1. Of course, there are many types of crabs, so the crabs in the tin shack may be an entirely different type.

your fingers bend. Remember that a crab has five limbs on each side of its body. So if five limbs, bending like your fingers, are moving all at once, it is natural that the crab is going to move sideways. Think about it, and you'll see what I mean.

But can the crabs actually adhere to the walls and ceiling? I have found no evidence of this possibility, though Mr. Snicket may know far more about crab biology than I do. Basically, I think it would be amusing if the orphans taught all those crabs how to do tricks. After all, people teach their dogs and cats to do tricks, so why can't people teach crabs to do tricks? Perhaps the main trick is to get the crabs to wade through a sticky substance, then race up the walls of the room. At some point, either the sticky substance would solidify, thus gluing the crabs to the walls and ceiling; or the sticky substance would wear off the crabs' limbs, and they would all fall from the ceiling onto the heads of the children.

In fact, if your tin shack is infested by crabs, it might make sense to smear a sticky substance on the walls, hoping the crabs will indeed get the glue on their limbs and eventually just stick to the ceiling, wither away, and die.

It would be very interesting if the shack were infested with larger crabs, such as Robber Crabs or Hermit Crabs. Robbers are bright red and orange, and Hermits hide in their big shells. If filled with Robbers, the shack would be rocking. It would glow so brightly that the orphans wouldn't be able to sleep, and the crabs would be scampering everywhere, making it nearly impossible to walk across the floor. If filled with Hermits, there would be mounds of Hermit shells everywhere, with terrified crabs hiding inside them. Either way, it's an odd image, indeed.

Second Up: Dripping Splotches of Fungi

What type of fungus—light tan, constantly dripping juice— is growing on the ceiling of the shack? To answer this question, we first have to know what is meant by fungus.

There's fungus that grows on your toes, fungus that grows in the yard, and fungus that you put on pizza. The fungus on your toes makes you itch, and your mother has to give you ointment to get rid of it. It's a scaly mess, red and white.

The fungus in the yard is in the form of all the mushrooms that pop up beneath trees and across fields of grass. These mushrooms are interconnected all across the lawn beneath the ground. If you pull one up, another pops up in its place. The only way to get rid of them is to rip out the entire networked system of mushrooms in the ground, which is a very difficult task.

The fungus on your pizza also happens to be mushrooms. They are known as *Agaricus bisporus*. If you really want to impress your teacher, or if you really want to get the pizza delivery guy mad, ask for a large pizza with extra *Agaricus bisporus*. Unlike the lawn mushrooms, which tend to be poisonous, the ones on your pizza are quite tasty. And, yes, they are fungus.

So how can all these really different things be fungus, the same thing?

First up, the plural of fungus is fungi, or more than one fungus. One mushroom on your pizza is a fungus. More than one mushroom, and your pizza is loaded with fungi.

The fungi are one of the five kingdoms of life. Each kingdom is then divided into phylums, classes, orders, families, genuses, and species.

The Monera kingdom contains the single-celled organisms without a nucleus. These organisms are also called prokaryotes and include bacteria and blue-green algae.

The Protoctista kingdom contains the simple eukaryotes, or single-celled organisms having a nucleus. Examples include slime molds and nucleated algae.

Aha, and now we reach the Fungi kingdom, the one with which we are most concerned right now. These organisms lack flagella and develop from spores. In addition to mushrooms, they include yeast and molds.

The Plantae kingdom is the plant kingdom: they use chlorophyll and include mosses and vascular plants.

The Animalia kingdom, or animal kingdom, contains you and me. These organisms are multicellular and develop from a blastula, which is a hollow ball of cells. They include worms and arthropods, as well as animals.

Notice that the fungi are more plantlike than animal. Yet they lack chlorophyll. It is because they lack chlorophyll that they often grow in dark, damp places. Not requiring light to make food, they can survive quite comfortably in the dark.

In general, the fungi have these characteristics:

- Eukaryotic, which means each cell has a distinct nucleus containing genetic material. Bacteria are not eukaryotic. Rather, a bacteria cell's genetic material is not enclosed in a nucleus. Instead, it is contained in one filament of DNA.
- Nonvascular, which means they do not have vessels, such as arteries or stems, that transport liquids.
- Reproduce with spores or by budding.
- Usually not motile, which means they cannot run down the street or climb a tree in some directed way. Motile implies that an organism can move in an independent and spontaneous way. So if the mushroom on your pizza could think, I will leap off this pizza and plunge myself into that kid's neck, the mushroom would be capable of motile movement. But mushrooms and other fungi cannot direct themselves to leap off tall buildings and attack wild beasts. The only way they can get somewhere else is to produce spores that then float through the air or travel through soil and liquid. Or produce buds that drop and roll somewhere else.
- May have microscopic threads (molds).
- May be unicellular, meaning the entire organism is made up of only one cell (yeasts).
- Have plantlike cell walls, but fungi cell walls are made mainly of chitin, while plant cell walls are made mainly of cellulose.
- Feed on preformed organic material rather than using photosynthesis to make their own food.
- Digest their food, then ingest it. People, by contrast, ingest or eat food, then digest it.

• Store food internally as glycogen, as animals do, whereas plants store food internally as starch.

There are more than a million species of fungi, according to the mycologists who study them. For example, the yeast fungus, *Saccharomyces cereviseae*, is used to make bread rise and to make the alcohol in beer. Other forms of fungi eat food from our trash, decompose the trash, and make it into soil.

Your toe fungus is called tinea, dermatomycosis, or simply, ringworm. Oddly enough, ringworm is not really a worm at all—not a squirmy, slimy worm. The type of fungus that gets on your body makes you itch, and it also makes you sneeze and cough. I am highly allergic to fungus. It makes my back itch, my neck, my scalp; it makes me sneeze constantly, and it makes my eyes water.

When fungi get into buildings, people can get very sick. These nasty fungi are called penicillium and stachybotrys. While it's possible that the tin shack is infected with penicillium and stachybotrys, I think it's unlikely, as these forms of fungi are microscopic and float in the air. The tin shack is infected with splotches of dripping, light tan fungus.

In many ways, fungi are harmful. In addition to getting into our air, as mentioned above, they cause diseases in humans and other animals, and also in crops and other plants. They rot and contaminate food. They can destroy all sorts of things, such as plastics and pesticides.

But in many ways, including pizza mushrooms, fungi are

good for us. They are used to bake and brew food and drink. They are used in antibiotics, such as penicillin. They are used in products such as colas, in medicines, and in certain cheeses, such as blue cheese and Roquefort.

The fungi are divided into major groups, yeasts and molds. Yeasts reproduce by budding or fission. Budding is when the yeast just grows a tiny new organism on itself, a bud that drops off to become its own organism. Fission is when the yeast cells just split, creating multiple yeast cells, each able to develop into entirely new, individual yeast organisms. Yeasts are usually moist, almost like mucous.

With the molds, they produce spores that produce long, branching filaments called hyphae. A mass of hyphae is called a mycelium.

As an aside, there is a small town in North Wales called Mold. The town is an ancient parish of a place called Flintshire. The ancient parish served the towns of Arddun-went, Argoed, Birchenald, Bistre, Broncoed, Cilrhedynnen, Groesonnen, Gwernaffield, Gwernymynydd, Gwysanau, Harts-heath, Hendebifa, Leeswood, Llai, Llong, Llwynegrin, Ner-cwys, Pantymwyn, Pontbleiddyn, Pentre, Rhual, Rhydgoli, Tre'r Beirdd, Treuddyn, and Waunyrwyddfid.[2]

But let's return to Prufrock Prep and the Baudelaires' tin shack. Let's try to determine what type of fungus is light tan

---

2. You can read a lot more about Mold at www.genuki.org.uk/big/wal/FLN/Mold and www.moldweb.co.uk.

and could drip constantly from a ceiling. Is the Baudelaire fungus a yeast? Or is a mold?

The type of yeast used to make bread, beer, and wine is a fungi known as *Saccharomyces cerevisiae*. This type of fungi grows quickly, and within a few days, you see a light tannish moist splotch of yeast. Not being a mold, they have no hyphae, or long filaments with spores. Rather, they are round or look like ellipses, and they reproduce by budding.

It is possible that this type of fungi is growing in the tin shack. They are light tan and moist, and if left long enough in the shack, might grow into a dripping splotch. Perhaps someone accidentally tossed a blob of pizza dough at the ceiling, and it adhered. Perhaps that blob then gave rise to the fungi. Perhaps someone was having a wild party complete with bread and beer, and beer splashed onto the ceiling, along with bread fragments, eventually giving rise to the fungi.

Anything's possible.

I think it's more likely, however, that the fungi growing in the shack is a form of mold. In my basement, a former resident stored a thousand pounds of ordinary cardboard boxes, all stuffed with papers and photographs. My basement happens to be over a hundred years old. The floor and walls are ancient stone. And it gets pretty damp down there. In fact, the old stone floor ranges from moist to wet. Over time, the cardboard boxes liquified on the wet floor. The tan boxes melted into pools of black slime. I could easily envision the black slime as tan slime, clinging to the ceiling down there, dripping endlessly.

Molds decompose other things.[3] That is how they eat. They travel as microscopic spores, and even outdoors, there may be 500 to 1,000 mold spores in every cubic meter of air. It's really easy for these microscopic spores to get inside your house, your school, the tin shack. And once inside, all they need are food, which can be a ceiling tile or some wall, and water to multiply.

Common indoor molds are aspergillus, alternaria, cladosporium, and penicillium. If on a tin ceiling, all they need is some dead organic material—hair, flies, crumbs, anything—and a little moisture to go wild and multiply and spread.

Now I wouldn't want to be sleeping under a mound of dripping aspergillus. It could cause infection and other illness. Besides, it's just gross stuff.

There are more than 185 species of aspergillus. Scientists already know that approximately twenty of the species cause infections in people. The most common infection-causing types are *Aspergillus fumigatus, Aspergillus flavus,* and *Aspergillus niger.* Some of the problems you may get if aspergillus is dripping on you are: sinusitis, myocarditis, meningitis, endocarditis, cerebral aspergillosis, pulmonary aspergillosis, osteomyelitis, endophthalmitis, cutaneous aspergillosis, hepatosplenic aspergillosis, and many others. You may either sneeze and itch, or your life may be threatened by the aspergillus.

---

3. If you've ever wondered, mildew is a common name for an enormous amount of mold.

Aspergillus range in color from blue-green to yellow-green to gray to purplish red to ... light tan. I have seen photographs of *Aspergillus terreus* and *Aspergillus nidulus*,[4] and the fungi definitely exists as a tan splotch.

If you have fungi growing in your shack, how do you get rid of it? Let's consider the black slime mold growing all over my basement floor. I really have to clean it up before it kills me. If I run the vacuum over the mess, then try to vacuum my bedroom, I'd blow mold spores everywhere and choke to death at night. (I tried this method, and, believe me, it's not the way to go.) If I moisten the mold further, then put bleach on it and mop up the mess, I'd be in much better shape. I wouldn't be blowing the spores all over my house. The poor Baudelaire orphans. I really feel sorry for them. All I have is black mold in the basement. They've got splotches of the junk dripping on their heads all night.

As a final note, it would be a lot more lovely for the orphans if the fungi in their shack were not light tan, dripping juice, and clinging to the ceiling. If, for example, the fungi was instead a bolete, it would be a gorgeous bushlike fungi, tan and looking kind of like coral, and maybe in a pot by the front door. Or, indeed, if they had an actual coral fungus, they'd have a beautiful bright red splash of coral in their pot

---

4. You can see these photographs, too, at pangloss.ucsf.edu/ ... rreussd2d5.4ofw4.jpg and pangloss.ucsf.edu/ ... idulussdd7.1ofw4.jpg, as well as many other Web sites.

by the door. On the other side of the door could be a poly-pore, which is bright blue and which spreads like a fan. For pure beauty in the shack, almost as good as watching goldfish in an aquarium, the orphans could have a craisin fungus, which is bright orange, growing like large, folded, raisin-like clumps on trees. The bright blue *Pulcherricium caeruleum* is smooth and glossy, and would be a much better choice for interior decoration than the plain light tan fungi splotch on the shack ceiling. Wouldn't you rather have a bright blue ceiling than a splotched light tan ceiling?

Third Up: Sunny's Staples

In Book the Fifth, *The Austere Academy*, Sunny manually makes staples, and soon her brother and sister are helping her. Who invented staples, and when? Were staples made by hand in the fifteenth century, as Duncan suggests? If you were forced to make staples manually, how would you do it?

Towards the end of the nineteenth century, magazines were bound by sewing all the pages together with a long piece of wire. Wire stitcher machines were very common in the book and magazine business. The wire was both the needle and the thread. Wire was used rather than cotton thread because wire is much stronger.

In 1896, a Boston inventor named Thomas Briggs created a stitching machine that could handle books and magazines of different sizes. By turning some screws, people could adjust the wire stitching for either huge volumes or slim pamphlets.[5] Briggs's company was known as the Boston Wire Stitcher Company.

The stitching machine fed wire into the book or magazine, then cut the wire, bending it into a U-shape. It clasped the wire into a stitch. The actual part of the machine that fed the wire into the material was pretty big, and the stitches were twelve inches apart. Obviously, multiple passes through the stitcher machine were necessary to bind a book or magazine with wire stitches that were closer than twelve inches from one another. Eventually Briggs invented another version of his machine that placed the stitches two inches apart.

Later, the machines were redesigned to use individual pieces of wires rather than long strands. The individual pieces meant that the machine did not have to cut the wire, then bend it. The individual pieces were already shaped so the machine only had to drive them into the book and clasp them. Guess what these individual pieces were called? *Staples.*

Actually, the staples used by the stitching machines were not the first known use of staples. That was in the 1200s, when short ribbons were twined through cuts in the upper left corners of papers. These ribbons were not called staples, but they served the same purpose.[6]

Later, wax and ribbon were used together to seal the pages

---

5. Henry Petroski, *The Evolution of Useful Things* (New York: Random House Vintage Books, 1992), p. 89.

6. See the Stapler Database at 24.97.84.9/stapler/history.htm.

more tightly. Much later, in the 1700s, people made staples by hand for King Louis XV in France. It wasn't until the late 1800s that the staplers or stitching machines were invented, and, finally, early in 1900, that strips of staples were made from sheet metal.

Today, staples come in a wide variety of metals, shapes, and sizes. You can get staples made from stainless steel, aluminum, and many other metals. There are staples with rounded tops, humped tops, square tops, and curved tops. Some are extremely wide and thick, others are very tiny and thin.

At Prufrock Prep, Sunny probably makes ordinary office staples. I suppose this could be done by bending short pieces of wire into appropriate shapes. The more interesting question, of course, is *why* anyone would force somebody else to make metal staples by hand. With the obvious answer being: sheer abusive brutality!

If forced to make staples by hand, I'd beg for a pair of pliers to bend the metal. I'd also beg for metal cutters, so I could cut the metal wires into small pieces. And a ruler would be handy to keep all the staples a uniform size.

Beyond that, I'd suggest that the evil monster forcing me to make staples switch to glue.

Last Up: Killer Leeches

Leeches are worms that suck your blood.

Let me pause for a moment, as I cannot resist . . .

If a leech is a worm that sucks your blood, then it could

be argued that bullies are leeches, bosses are leeches, and creepy people who latch onto you and try to live off you are leeches.

Suppose your Uncle Jasper moves into your house, and your mother thinks he's going to stay for only a couple of days. But Uncle Jasper never leaves. Nor does he have a job. Uncle Jasper eats your food, runs up your electric bill (watching television all day while your mother works and you're in school), and even takes over your bedroom. In fact, it gets so bad that you are forced to sleep on the hard wood floor in the living room, while Uncle Jasper snores and slobbers in your bed. Uncle Jasper is a leech.

After a year, your mother hires a lawyer to dispose of Uncle Jasper. The lawyer wears extremely expensive suits, and her children attend the fanciest private schools. Your mother, on the other hand, wears tattered blue jean coveralls and you attend the worst school in town. The lawyer charges your mother two hundred dollars per hour. Instead of getting rid of Uncle Jasper, the lawyer maneuvers your life so that you must actually pay Uncle Jasper ten thousand dollars! In addition, for this "service," the lawyer charges your mother six thousand dollars. You and your mother end up living on the street in a box under the railroad tracks. Uncle Jasper takes the ten thousand dollars and buys his own house, one right next to the lawyer. And the lawyer, among other things, is a major blood-sucking leech.

Now, in reality, the creature scientifically known as a leech is not much different from Uncle Jasper and the lawyer. A flattened water bug of approximately thirty-four body segments, the leech has sensory organs on its head and body that enable it to notice changes in temperature and vibration. It also has chemical receptors on its head that give it a sense of smell. And it may have numerous eyes.

The leeches in Lake Lachrymose are particularly gruesome. An entire "swarm" of Lachrymose Leeches attacks the sailboat in which Violet, Klaus, Sunny, and Aunt Josephine are escaping. The leeches knock against the wood of the sailboat, trying to eat it, then swim away *en masse* (which means "all at the same time"), only to swivel quickly and then zoom madly back. They are so powerful that they crack a hole in the boat.

Now leeches are hideous things, but they don't gang up on sailboats, smashing against them as if playing a football game; and their teeth aren't so incredibly powerful that they can eat holes into the sides of boats.

Instead, to eat, leeches use their suckers. On each end of its body, the leech has a sucker. The front sucker drinks blood, the rear sucker helps the leech move. The leech is a parasite, meaning it attaches itself to other animals and literally sucks the life out of them. The other animals get sick and die. After all, animals cannot live without their blood.

Some leeches digest muscles rather than drink blood. Some leeches do both: they dissolve the body tissues of a snail, for example, and then for dessert, drink the blood out of a frog.

Most leeches have strong, semicircular jaws containing many teeth. When a leech bites into a victim, it makes its body rigid and holds its sucker firmly in place. It uses its toothed jaws like sawblades to make incisions into the victim's skin. The leech then excretes mucous from its nepro-pores, which are openings from the leech's kidney-type organs. The mucous glues the sucker to the victim. (Is this gross enough for you? I'm writing this section while eating breakfast, and, frankly, I'm choking on my doughnut.) At this point, the leech floods the wound with saliva containing painkillers so the victim is unlikely to notice that a leech is attached to him; and an anticoagulant called hirudin that keeps the victim's blood from scabbing. (I'm now putting the doughnut aside. I'll have to leave the room for a few minutes and try not to get sick. Let me get some fresh air . . .)

(Okay, I think that I can continue now. If you feel sick while reading this section of the book, I recommend that you [a] not eat anything, and [b] suck some—oops, I mean, breathe some—fresh air.)

Let's return to the delightful leech, sure to make a great pet for any boy or girl, better than a dog or cat, better than a bird or goldfish. The delightful leech can sit in a filthy-water aquarium in your very own living room. It can leave blood trails all over the glass sides of the aquarium, thrilling both friends and family with interesting streak patterns. The leech can entertain at social gatherings, such as parties:

watch the pet leech suck dry a toad or your former pet gold-fish.

Yes, the delightful leech can drink and contain five times its own body weight in blood. If a leech weighs 3 ounces, for example, it can drink 15 ounces of blood at a single time. This is better than Dracula! If he weighs two hundred pounds (or 3,200 ounces), there's no way the old vampire can drink 16,000 ounces of blood at one time.

Now let's suppose a leech smells you and rams its sucker into your leg. Eventually, you notice that your leg is shrinking and aching. You look down, and, oh no, there it is: the leech. What do you do? Your first thought is to rip that sucker off your body. But you don't want to do that. While you may be able to rip off most of the leech, its mouthparts will remain inside your skin, causing serious in-fections.

Instead, hobble to your nearest responsible adult and point to the leech on your leg. With as little hysteria as possible, note that your leg is now one-half its normal size and has ab-solutely no color in it. Tell the adult *not* to rip the leech off your leg. Tell the adult to get salt, matches, and maybe pins.

Salt sometimes works to get leeches off skin. And if you're desperate, have somebody use a hot pin or a lit match to force the leech off your body. Most definitely, do not light matches on your body. Make sure to have your parent, a teacher, or another responsible adult take care of it for you. If you do not know any responsible adults, then I suppose you might have to get a pound of salt and rub it on the leech and your wound until the worm keels over.[7]

Most definitely, a leech can kill a person, if not by blood-sucking alone, then certainly by causing deadly infections. And, yes, they can also smell you coming closer to them. I can't emphasize enough how creepy these worms are—

Leeches breathe through their skin. They live in darkness: under rocks, hidden in dense plant growths, in dirty water. Though some leeches live on land and in saltwater, most live in fresh water, meaning ponds, streams, lakes, and similar places. When they sense movement in the water, or when they smell something, leeches become excited: prey must be near. If the water dries up or grows cold in winter, the leeches bury themselves in the mud and hibernate for months. If they drink enough blood—say, five times their body weight in blood—they can go for an entire year without feeding again.

Many species of leeches thrive in the world.[8] Most have

---

7. These techniques may also work on ticks. When I was five years old, the man who lived in the house behind ours went hunting and got hundreds of ticks in his legs. Doctors tried removing the ticks with lit matches and other forms of heat, but nothing worked. Basically, the guy just had too many ticks in his legs, and eventually, he died from blood loss and infection. It was extremely creepy. His daughter was my best friend.

8. For example, in New Zealand and Australia alone, there are approximately ninety-eight species of leeches. For more details, see the list compiled by Dr. Fredric R. Govedich of Monash University School of Biological Sciences at www.personal.monash.edu.au/~fgodevic/leech/LIT.

Weird Leech Facts

1. Throughout history, women and children earned food and other critical items by wading barelegged into leech-infested ponds. They essentially worked as leech harvesters.

2. Leeches are hermaphrodites, meaning that each leech has both male and female reproductive organs.

3. There are 650 species of leeches.

4. The European medicinal Hirudo leech has three jaws, each with 100 teeth. Each leech has a total of 300 teeth.

5. While marching from Egypt across the Sinai Peninsula to Syria in 1799, Napoleon's soldiers drank leech-contaminated water. Talk about gross: the leeches were all over the insides of the men's bodies: in their mouths, throats, noses, and stomachs. The leeches began to suck the men's blood, and many men suffocated because blood-engorged leeches were filling their throats. Napoleon lost a lot of soldiers.

6. In the 1959 movie *Attack of the Giant Leeches*,[9] a moonshine-swilling trapper dies from giant sucker wounds. In fact, a lot of people start dying from giant sucker wounds. When one guy forces his ex-wife and

---

9. Directed by Bernard L. Kowalski and written by Leo Gordon, the 1959 *Attack of the Giant Leeches* was released under several other names, such as *Attack of the Blood Leeches*, *She Demons of the Swamp*, and *The Giant Leeches*.

her boyfriend into the swamp, both die from leech attacks, and the guy hangs himself. Game wardens and local doctors eventually realize that gigantic leeches are behind all the deaths and that these leeches live in caves beneath the swamp. They blow up the caves using dynamite, and all the human-sized leeches are destroyed.

7. And now back to the gross stuff: In 1985, Dr. Joseph Upton sewed the ear back onto a five-year-old boy's head. Although the arteries were fine, smaller veins became congested with blood after four days. Dr. Upton stuck twenty-four leeches on the boy's ear. The leeches saved the boy's ear, so the story has a nice ending, though I bet it was pretty horrible to be the boy with the twenty-four leeches sucking blood out of his ear.

8. In the nineteenth century, French doctors used more than a billion leeches per year to cure every ill imaginable, including "bad humor."

three jaws and make Y-shaped incisions in their victims. Some have two jaws, such as the Australian land leech, which makes a V-shaped incision. With all their differences, leeches are grouped into four basic types:

- **Type 1.** These leeches are approximately 2.9 inches (or 7.5 centimeters) long. They are light gray, and they eat a lot of snails, which also happen to be light gray.

- **Type 2.** These leeches are also about 2.9 inches long, are dark gray and black, and drink the blood of fish, frogs, water bugs, and humans.

- **Type 3.** These bad boys suck the blood from humans. Covered with red and black spots and sporting green racecar stripes on top and orange-brown on their undersides, these ugly suckers also drink the blood of fish, amphibians, birds, and other mammals. They drink the blood of just about anything that moves.

- **Type 4.** These leeches can grow up to 15 inches long. Grey with blotches, they drink the blood of living creatures as well as the blood of the dead. If the blood smells good enough, they come out of the water to feed.

For more than two thousand years, leeches have been used to remove blood from medical patients. Yes, I kid you not: doctors use leeches for bloodletting. Today's plastic surgeons may use leeches when their patients have a lot of blood beneath skin and muscle flaps. Leeches are also used when treating black eyes.[10] If you can stomach more leech horrors, take a look at "Weird Leech Facts" (pages 181-182).

---

10. Personally, I'd wear an eye patch before I'd let anybody stick a leech in my eye.

CHAPTER FOURTEEN

I Want to Be Someone Else

This is a critical chapter in this critical book about the Lemony Snicket universe. Let's face it: every Lemony Snicket book hinges on the fact that Count Olaf is a master of disguise. He is Stephano, Captain Sham, Shirley the receptionist, Coach Genghis (Khan), Gunther, and Detective Dupin.

In real life, how does a master of disguise operate? How does he remain undetected? How can you legally change your identity, not once, but multiple times? That is, if Count Olaf is able to obtain a job as a teacher, he must supply his name, driver's license, college graduation information, job history, and other important facts. Does he counterfeit this information? What types of counterfeiting tools do real masters of disguise use? Burning questions, as we delve into a key plot device used in all Lemony Snicket books.

First, it's hard to imagine that nobody would realize that Count Olaf is Stephano, Captain Sham, Shirley the receptionist, Coach Genghis (Khan), Gunther, and Detective Dupin: all the same guy. Especially when you consider that he assumes these disguises over a short period of time. As soon as he ditches one disguise, Count Olaf assumes another.

It's easy to put on a different pair of pants, a wig, a fake mustache, some lipstick, glasses, a hat, a skirt, a pair of high heels. It's not so easy to disguise facial hair when pretending to be Shirley. It's not so easy to become fatter or thinner, shorter or taller. And given how quickly Count Olaf changes his identity over the course of the Snicket books, it's safe to assume that he doesn't have time for plastic surgery, heavy eating, or starvation dieting.

In short, there's just so much Count Olaf can do to alter his physical appearance from one month to the next.

So we have to set this issue aside, and just ride with the fun of the Lemony Snicket universe. We have to assume that Count Olaf's wigs are so superior, that his hair dye is so radically awesome, that his legs are so male yet female, that he looks great in pants yet great in a skirt, that his voice can change at whim to sound like multiple people—we have to assume all of this and more to enjoy his impersonations. I don't know about you, but I had no trouble playing along with Lemony Snicket and laughing at the Count's crazy getups and impersonations. I kept thinking, "Why don't you guys [the orphans] know who he is? Why don't you realize that he's Count Olaf and run away quickly, *very* quickly?"

As for changing his identity legally, that's not very hard to do, at all. Being a modern criminal, Count Olaf obviously knows how to forge his identity using fake driver's licenses, passports, bank accounts, and so forth.

In fact, identity theft is more common than you might think. In 1999, the U.S. government Social Security Administration's Fraud Hotline received 62,000 reports of identity theft involving social security numbers.[1] In 1997, TransUnion Corporation, a credit bureau (meaning they keep track of all of your parents' purchases, credit card transactions, and other financial transactions), reported that two-thirds of the inquiries to its fraud department were related to identity theft. This percentage amounted to 43,000 allegations of identity theft per month.[2] There have been cases of

---

1. Sean B. Hoar, U.S. Department of Justice, Executive Office for United States Attorneys. "Identity Theft: The Crime of the New Millennium," *USA Bulletin*, March 2001, p. 1.

2. Robert Hammond, *Identity Theft: How to Protect Your Most Valuable Assets* (Franklin Lakes, New Jersey: Career Press, 2003), p. 20.

guys selling social security numbers on eBay, a hospital employee selling the identities of 393 hospital patients; and even a case involving an identity theft gang that assumed the identities of senior citizens in order to sell the old folks' houses for large amounts of cash.[3]

If Count Olaf steals other peoples' identities, he can be Stephano one month, Captain Sham the next, and Coach Genghis the third. It could be as simple as stealing Stephano's mail, specifically a credit card statement or offer to buy a credit card; submitting a change of address form for Captain Sham, then picking up Sham's mail somewhere else to obtain credit card and bank account information, boat-ownership information, and medical records; rooting through Genghis Khan's trash to get psychiatric reports and prescriptions for psychiatric drugs.

At this point, Count Olaf need only open new credit cards in the names of Stephano, Sham, and Genghis; use their current credit cards to run up bills; get phones installed using their personal information; open bank accounts in their names to write phony checks that eventually bounce; buy cars and other expensive items, such as boats.

To protect his real identity, Count Olaf could further cover his tracks. To do this, he could use an unlisted telephone and never supply his real mailing address to anybody.

---

3. Attorney General John Ashcroft, Identity Theft Press Conference transcript, May 2002, as reported in ibid., p. 24.

He would only use mailboxes set up by companies. This type of mailbox has a real address associated with it—not just a P.O. box address. But rather than being a mailbox on your apartment building or house, it is a box inside a storefront location. The storefront is usually accessible 24 hours a day, 7 days of the week, and if Olaf gets his mail in the middle of the night, nobody ever knows he's been there, who he is, or what type of mail he's getting.

Next, he can list his utilities under a series of phony names (all obtained through identity theft). Utilities are things like electricity, gas, and water bills. Even his license plates can be registered under these phony names using phony addresses. He would cancel all magazine and newspaper subscriptions. He would not go to church (well, *duh!*), and he would not join hobby clubs (yeah, *no kidding!*).

He would shred all his mail, as well as any papers that could possibly indicate his true identity. This is the sort of thing, as are all the other measures I've just listed, that real identity thieves do.

The only hitch I see to all of this is that for Count Olaf to get jobs wherever the orphans end up means that he must supply his social security number and driver's license to his employers. Let's face it. Employers always require you to give them your social security number and driver's license, and with jobs so scarce these days, anybody who wants to work absolutely must cough up this private data. Else, you don't get the job.

So how does Count Olaf hide if they have this kind of information about him? He must use phony social security numbers and driver's licenses. He either steals identities, as mentioned earlier, or he dummies up his own documents. This is commonly known as forgery, and I do not recommend that you try it. It happens to be against the law, and if you try it, you could end up being like Count Olaf, or worse, get caught (which Count Olaf has yet to do, but I'm pretty sure he's going to get what's coming to him in one of these books) and go the slammer for the rest of your life. Now I don't know what you think about spending fifty years in the slammer, but it doesn't sound like much fun to me. Sure, you get free food, but it makes your school cafeteria food look and taste like a fine roast beef dinner au jus (that means the cow juice rather than fake canned gravy) with chocolate cake for dessert. Sure, you get a private room all to yourself, but—need I point this out?—it's really tiny, enclosed in steel bars, and has a smelly open toilet next to the bed. Sure, you don't have to go to school again, but, on the other hand, you're not allowed to go anywhere else, either, not even into the hall. And if you're a girl, the clothes aren't exactly the kind of stuff you see on Christina or Britney. If you're a guy, you're not exactly going to be a chick magnet in the slammer . . . um, where there are no chicks to magnetize.

So now that I've dissuaded you (which means persuaded you from *not* doing something) from pursuing a professional life of forgery, we can tackle the final, really big question about Count Olaf's use of multiple identities. How does he get the fake IDs?

In short, he must be a forger or he must have a forger-buddy. The forger obtains notary stamps and seals, and he falsifies the documents required by state agencies that issue driver's licenses. All he needs is the correct type of paper and ink, a computer, and a cheap computer scanner/printer. Once the forger has a fake driver's license, he can obtain social security numbers as well. But here's another, much simpler method of obtaining a fake ID.

The bad guy dresses like a normal guy in a clown suit, long beard, and bikini on his head. Well, no, I take that back. He dresses like a normal guy in jeans and a sweatshirt, something like that. He goes to the mall or to a carnival. He gets all flustered and tells a policeman that he's just been robbed. He claims that the robber stole his wallet. When the policeman asks the bad guy for his name and address, that sort of thing, the bad guy gives phony information that subsequently goes on the police report.

The bad guy takes the police report to the Department of Motor Vehicles, where he asks for a new driver's license. The bad guy explains that he has to get new credit cards to replace the ones that were stolen from him, which he had to cancel right away. The bad guy further claims to be from another state. He needs a place to stay that night, and no hotel will give him a room without a driver's license. When the Department of Motor Vehicles guy looks in the computer records, he won't find the forger due to the supposed out-of-state address. Sometimes, the bad guy gets a driver's license right then and there, just taking the written test. Sometimes, he must return the next day and take a driving test, too. But, regardless, the bad guy usually gets a fake ID using this method. And once he has the fake driver's license, he can get most anything else that he wants.

It's probably a lot easier, overall, to steal someone else's identity, if indeed you are inclined to be a bad guy and don't mind the risk of spending the next fifty years behind bars. And I think that this is exactly what Count Olaf does. He Dumpster dives, he finds credit card bills and other interesting trash. He steals identities from a bunch of people. He moves from town to town every month. Nobody ever knows his real name. It might not be Count Olaf. Instead, it might be Master Sergeant Sergio Van Trunkelthorpe.

Speaking of such things, how do you know that I am really Lois H. Gresh? How do you know that you are looking at my photo at the end of the book? Perhaps I'm really Lemony Snicket. Perhaps he's really me. Perhaps I'm really your principal, your teacher, your friend's father, your pet dog. Perhaps I'm not even real. Perhaps this entire book was written by (dreadfully malfunctioning) computer software.

Anything is possible. It's even possible that you liked this book.

You are now the world's leading expert on Lemony Snicket books. You know all about orphans and whether Count Olaf could marry fourteen-year-old Violet. You now know whether it's possible to be allergic to peppermints. You know more than you ever wanted to know about leeches, crabs, and fungi. You can hypnotize people. You may even have guessed the meaning behind Count Olaf's eyeball tattoo. Hot-air balloons, noisy shoes: you know it all.

You have now finished reading the Ultimate Book Report about Lemony Snicket. Why don't you try to write your own Snicket book report? And while you're conjuring up a book report, Lois H. Gresh (if indeed that is my real name) has to start writing another book. I think this new book will be *The Science of James Bond* (if indeed that is his real name). In fact, that very book is due in five months, and I've yet to watch a single Bond movie to analyze the details behind the Bond supermodern scientific gizmos. I've been so immersed in Lemony Snicket that, for many months, I've not eaten (anything but pizza and doughnuts), not shaved my whiskers (but then, I'm female), not slept (except twelve hours a day), and not seen my friends (assuming I have any).

I anxiously await the next Snicket book. At this time, there are only ten Snicket books, featuring Violet, Klaus, and Sunny Baudelaire. *Bring on the eleventh!* I say. We're dying to read it. We can wait no longer!

Will it take place in a coal mine, in a cola factory, on a coffee plantation, in a monkey-hippo-hybrid breeding laboratory? What disguise will Count Olaf assume this time? Will he be a diving coach off the coast of Labrador, or will he be a breeder of rare Cane Corso dogs?

Perhaps he'll be a breeder of Labrador Retrievers who

doubles as a diving coach off the coast of Labrador. Only time will tell.

And until that time, I'll amuse myself by practicing paper-clip lock picking, studying leeches, and building aqua-terrariums for my ghost and zombie shrimp. I'll limp through the woods, seeking weird, dripping fungi. I'll make sea cucumber sandwiches. And I'll dream about Beagan, the small man who danced at the fire hall: love forever, once desired, love forever, and then he expired.

Lois H. Gresh is the author of eleven horrible books. She's been falsely accused of trapping canaries in coal mines, forging Eye of Horus amulets in Cairo, and casting the Evil Eye upon entire cities, including Paris, London, New York, Tokyo, and Budapest. She has been correctly accused of murdering thousands of hornets and wasps. She currently lives in an igloo, but with her profits from writing this book, she plans to move to a grass hut near the equator.

You can visit her Web site at www.sff.net/people/lgresh.